Namasta
Liz —
Here's to
feeling fit ☺

Brad

WORDS FOR THE SOUL

Heaven-Sent Life Lessons
& Conversations with God

Volume 1

A Soul-Felt Sequel™

Spiritual Short Stories

Written By:

The Corporate Woo-Woo™

Michelle Skaletski-Boyd CHt

"Enjoy the Experience" ™

A Publication Creation by
Soul-Felt Words, Inc.
www.soul-felt.com

Copyright © Soul-Felt Words, Inc.,
All rights reserved.
Print Edition 2015
ISBN: 978-0-9903017-3-8

Cover Design by Cory Wright
Interior Design by Wes Thomas

1) Body, Mind & Spirit 2) Prayer 3) Spirituality

A Soul-Felt Author Message

Namaste ~ This greeting means the spirit in me honors the spirit in you. The light in me recognizes the light in you. A soul-felt thank you for meeting me here on the path.

Each lesson in this book is based on my own experience with God, also called Creator, Higher Power, Infinite Source, Divine Wisdom, and so on. Please choose that which feels best to you.

Throughout every lesson, soul-felt words are sprinkled in to help you better understand your Self. Word definitions are cited from Webster's New Universal Unabridged Dictionary, 2001, Barnes & Noble, Inc./Random House, Inc. (referred to as 'Webster's throughout this book for ease and simplicity).

Once you've completed a story, please take plenty of time to allow the message to marinate as it begins to safely travel through your subconscious mind.

To get the most from every spiritual story, chapters are listed in linear order for those who think more logically. Dates are given for those who are curious about the chain of events. A category section is also available to make this more fun and experiential. Muscle test, use your intuition, and/or ask your spiritual team for some assistance so you can "land on" the perfect story at this time.

Everything listed is for educational purposes only and is not intended nor should be construed as any other services or advice.

As always, your truth is your own so please discern each lesson for your Self because just as Plato implied, one cannot know anything with absolute certainty yet one can feel confident about certain things.

May you Enjoy the Experience ™ along the way,
~ Michelle

Dedication

A soul-felt thank you to Source, whom I call God, for giving me the power and the beauty of co-creation.

A huge hug to my inner-sphere, to include my dear spouse Steven and to my family and my friends both in the physical and heavenly realms for giving me the courage and the insight to make the leap.

Much appreciation to Wes Thomas and Mark Cloyd Martillan for working so wonderfully on this creation while assisting with its birth.

And a special note of gratitude to you, dear reader, for allowing me to create this space so you may fully connect to your Higher Self.

Enjoy the Experience ™

Table of Contents
(by category)

The Power Of Appreciation

The Art Of Surrender

Self-Acceptance And Perception

Moving Through Fears

Projection And Self-Reflection

Self-Trust And Confidence

CHILD'S PLAY

Change & Transformation

About The Author   133

AWAKEN TO YOUR SELF

"A single event can awaken within us a stranger totally unknown to us. To live is to be slowly born."

~ Author, Antoine de Saint-Exupéry

It's nearly 50 degrees today with promises of even higher temps tomorrow.

A couple of days ago I walked down to the river to breathe in the pleasant sights and sounds of the remaining melting snow.

Flocks of geese were migrating overhead as sweet singing robins joyously appeared along with magnificent rays of the sun.

How beautiful it is to be aware and to be still.

A little later in the day, I flipped on the local weather. The forecaster remarked, "Daylight savings time will unfortunately mean losing an hour this season."

I flicked off the channel and reprogrammed his words.

Moving our clocks ahead will not mean a loss. It will mean a gain.

A gain of more sunshine means more light, and with more light, comes a longer lasting awakening.

I know. I know. Some of you may think, "But we WILL 'lose' a whole hour of sleep."

Literally, yes you are right, yet rather than look at this through the hands of time, I prefer to view this from a spiritual perspective.

Awaken means "to come or bring to awareness." (Webster's)

The more you are awake, the more you come to know, so it's okay if you are still wondering, "Just what in the world is she talking about?"

When you are ready to awaken I am confident your imaginary fears will begin to disappear, and you'll start to challenge your old conditioned thinking, have a deeper recognition of your inner-voice, and feel much like a bear coming out of hibernation – craving the sweetness of understanding.

Personally, I'm now at a point where I feel more aware and recognize more, yet I am not yet able to sustain it. I awaken and then fall back to sleep, much like a baby needing naps.

I sense a new transition around the corner and do my best to enjoy this moment now, knowing it will hopefully get to a time when I will stop slipping back into old conditioned ways and stay firmly connected to my truth.

I remember watching Oprah Winfrey interview author, Eckhart Tolle in a 10 part on-line series. He described an awakening as an ultimate shift in consciousness.

To paraphrase something Eckhart said, we are not our

thought processes or the voices in our head. We are not our conditioning. We are not the future and we are not the past. When we make peace with the moment . . . when we accept, rather than resist, we are ready to be awakened, and the access point is NOW.

Spiritual awakening begins from within.

And consciously I choose to start my day by not just rousing myself from sleep but to fully awaken in the present moment by tapping into all of my senses and celebrating another day.

When I reach for my tea cup in the morning, I intentionally feel for the ceramic handle so it rests against my fingers; I listen to the steamy water as it whistles, then inhale the sweet smell of chamomile; I watch the calming liquid flow beautifully into my cup and allow its happy flavour to swirl upon my taste buds and satisfy my tongue.

ETE = Enjoy the Experience™
Lesson learned March 8, (year 2)

"DAM"-ING YOUR SELF

"The first step to change is awareness.
The second step is acceptance."

Nathaniel Branden

I spent most of last week unconscious of my own resistance. I could feel myself struggling with so many things.

It was as if personal awareness had been hi-jacked by my ego, leaving me with no memory of presence at all.

It started with a mental struggle when I learned that my new online newsletter software was less reliable than the first.

After spending hours converting over to a new system, I begrudgingly learned that I could no longer communicate to over half of my online subscribers.

My only choice was to learn from the experience and reinstall another system once again.

Yet, I did it with much resistance.

Rather than allow things to be what they were, I started losing a lot of sleep over it.

?

- What would people think?
- How incompetent this looked?
- Why couldn't things be easier?

On and on it went.

I was completely consumed in fearful thoughts and became very frustrated and upset.

My blindness to the truth caused me to be so unaware, that my sneaky ego fed off the pain.

All of the signs were there.

I was sneezing and tired and cranky and irritable and completely stuck in my head.

If only I had taken a moment to be present and allowed things "to be" while fully accepting.

Acceptance is "the act of taking or receiving something offered"; "favorable reception." (Webster's)

The problem was, I wasn't willingly receiving that which life had to offer. Instead, I was trying to stop the inevitable like a charging bull ramming its head at every circumstance and depleting myself of all energy.

It wasn't until dinner one evening that I finally became conscious again.

"You woke me in the middle of the night saying 'Dam, Dam, Dam' over and over again, my husband, Steve announced.

"I did?" I embarrassingly giggled. "What was that about?"

"You're obviously stressing out."

Was this the reason I had come down with a horrible head cold and felt like my sinuses were going to explode?

Was this why every little thing Steve did lately was grating on my nerves?

Was this happening because I had made ZERO time this week for meditation?

Just asking my Self these three questions pulled me back to center.

In fact, it seemed our Golden Retriever Buddy's recovery from surgery had become my "excuse" to give up on my daily walks, and, yes, negative thoughts had become so consuming that I had fallen sick with a cold.

Even sitting quietly in a chair lately had become too much of a chore.

Steve began clearing the table when suddenly I felt very compelled to stand with my arms akimbo and my head held high.

I walked to the center of the room and twirled myself in a circle around the shiny laminate floor. A tremendous wave of pent up energy moved through my being as I envisioned sticks in a beaver dam giving way. Then my Higher Power spoke through me aloud,

"Stop damming your Self and move out of the way!"

The voice was my own, but the words were not. They shot through me like a cannon ball, and I didn't know whether to laugh or to cry.

"When you feel like you are damming yourself, it's because you have," I consciously declared.

Steve's eyes glistened, as he knowingly smiled.

What a beautiful lesson to learn!

ETE = Enjoy the Experience™
Lesson learned May 17, (year 2)

A SPIRITUAL DETOUR

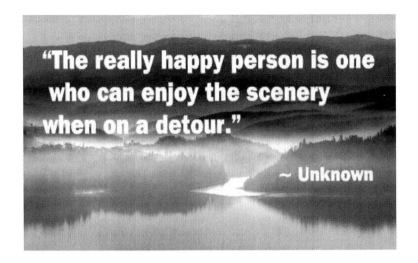

"The really happy person is one who can enjoy the scenery when on a detour."

~ Unknown

Throughout the week, my spiritual path has led me to some pretty big barriers.

I could feel stress take over my body like an invasive parasite.

Each unfinished project felt like a heavy stack of bodily bricks.

I had swollen glands, a tense jaw, knotted shoulders and a stiffening neck.

It wasn't until I was talking to my Canadian friend, Victory, that things finally started becoming clear.

"How are you able to juggle all of your projects without having a coronary," I teased.

"I use to hang on to all my ideas until everything was perfect," Victory admitted, "But, what I came to realize is that nothing ever is.

Things would pile up, and I'd get more and more stressed. Then, one day I was talking to my personal coach who said, 'Don't get it right. Just get it going.' I've lived by these words every since."

"I can use that," I smiled.

"I'm glad," Victory said. "Whenever you get inspired, move along on your project as far as you can go and then release it and see where it goes."

I began to practice this concept the next day.

My business was transferring my website over to a new web host provider, and things weren't going very smooth.

Domains were pointing to the wrong pages, databases were down, and people were calling to tell me emails were bouncing left and right.

I could feel the stress beginning to bubble. But, then I remembered to simply allow it to be.

Obstacles appear on our spiritual path for a reason.

They're here to serve us in a positive way.

Once I began to see this perceived "negative" energy differently, I was able to treat it like a friend.

Had I done everything I could possibly do in this very moment?

Yes, indeed.

I had contacted both my old and new web host providers alerting them to the issue, and I had thanked everyone who called and politely explained the situation.

Yet wait.

There was still one more thing... It was important I find joy in the moment.

I playfully stepped outside into the warm radiant sun to inhale deeply and look within. A spiritual detour then appeared.

A new way of thinking emerged.

Though not yet perfect, simply getting a revised website online has caused my business so much traffic momentum that people are now alerting me when my website is down.

This is a very good thing!

A detour is "a round about or circuitous way or course, especially one used temporarily when the main route is closed." (Webster's)

And so the lesson goes, when something doesn't go exactly as it should, take a spiritual detour in your mind, allow things to be as they are, and see the positive purpose in every direction. Because even obstacles are there to serve you well.

Here's to joy on your journey and peace on your mind!

ETE = Enjoy the Experience ™
Lesson learned May 3, (year 2)

LIVING ON THE EDGE

Passion is defined as "strong or extravagant fondness; a powerful or compelling emotion; an instance or experience of strong love." - (Webster's)

I had an amazingly adventurous week and am happy to live to tell about it.

On Tuesday I ventured out with five others to partake in one of the most intense adrenaline rushes of my life! The last time I felt so alive was when Steve and I rode our motorcycle over 8000 miles on a 3 week vacation.

Allow me to paint the picture . . .

There were six rookies, including me, and two experienced guides about to climb a Montana mountain on separate snowmobiles. It was my first time riding the powder on a sled, and let me tell you the accumulation this close to Canada was reaching record highs.

It was a snow-machining dream!

I hopped on a 4-stroke 660 Arctic Cat, and though some might say this was a baby in terms of cc's, this mountain cat was a much bigger breed than this mid-western gal was ever used to seeing.

The first few minutes were spent at the base of the mountain just a few miles from Steve and my parcel of land. It was time to get a feel of our new machine. After a short training session, all the sleds lined up for a fun drag race across a 20 acre field. Since my sled was the only electric start, I took the lead, and then quickly learned luxury has its trade off. The heavy weight of the 2-seater bogged me down so much that I fell behind the rest of the pack, and as I turned to circle toward the finish line the long tracks of the snowmobile sunk me deeply into slush.

The only line I would be crossing was the icy mire of a beaver pond. – Seriously? Thank goodness I'm getting better at public humiliation.

It took both guides to dig me out, and after we all had a good laugh about it, we headed up the mountain to try out some of the widely groomed trails.

The tracks ran nicely along the smooth terrain, and I grew more confident in my abilities.

Then, a series of moguls appeared, and though each bump was a fun one, I felt like I was riding the waves in a speedboat and catching too much air.

Thankfully, I let off the throttle just as the trails became un-groomed.

Then one of the guides motioned for us to form a single file; another took the tail. I was just in front of him.

Just like the elevation, the weather soon took a turn.

A heavy fog rolled in. The glare of the snow, the mist and the brume began to blend as one.

My pulse quickened as distress made its presence known.

Visibility was down to just 10 feet ahead, and the sled in front of me was kicking up so much powder that I opted to decelerate then watched as its blurry tail-lights darkened to a shadow and then fully disappeared.

I slowed to a snail's pace until I could finally see, but when I looked in my rear view mirror, the guide who was behind me was nowhere in sight.

Unbeknownst to me, he had darted through the trees, leaving me all alone in the spooky haze of the woods.

Then, just like an egg being divided between its white and its yolk, I could feel my soul separate from my body as the amygdala in my brain began believing the illusions that tag along with fear.

Was I going to die out here?

Even though my hands continued to control the levers, I was unable to see the trail. It was like riding the tracks of a train on the edge of a cliff, hoping and praying you wouldn't derail.

"Hey Beautiful," I heard telepathically.

It was the familiar voice of Tom — a long-time friend of Steve's who had just passed away last year.

Was he here to tell me my time was finally up?

My heart raced faster, and then I mentally replied. "Tom, is that really you?"

"It's really me," he comforted, "and Corey's here too."

Familiar chills ran up my spine.

Corey and Tom had been the best of friends as long as I could remember, but four years before Tom's death, Corey had departed this world as well.

"How are you doing?" Corey chimed in.

Hearing these kind voices from the past helped me realize they weren't sent to take me away but were here to help me face my fears.

Strange as this may sound, Corey and Tom were both snowmobile enthusiasts who had lived and died by their passion. They both died on a snowmobile and wouldn't have had it any other way.

I admit knowing this caused me more fear in that I wondered if my end was near. Yet, I also knew that if anyone could keep me safely on course, these two passionate sled-heads would be the ones to do it. I tried to stay focused on that.

My snowmobile continued to robotically move as it crept its way through the blinding mist and heavy snow.

I was terrified, and just when I thought I could take it no more, I saw the closest guide's headlights come into view.

Seeing his presence was like a beacon in the night, pointing me back to the group.

Not yet even half way through the ride, Corey and Tom assured me they would remain by my side.

I began to relax a little more when the group of sleds in front quickly screeched to a halt.

We had reached the highest point of elevation, and the icy snow was whipping sideways. The snow was so deep and so heavy that even the lead guide was unable to safely blaze a trail without the help of his colleague.

"Cut your engines," the lead guide yelled. "We'll be back in 15 minutes. We need to see if there's a safe way to get everyone down. If not, we'll have to turn around and come back the way we came."

I hugged my fingers to the last of the heat piping through the hand warmers then slowly turned off the key.

My friend Ron, who had been riding in front of me got off his sled and brushed himself off.

"This is nuts," he shouted.

"I agree," I laughed, "but it's also a little fun."

Ron grabbed his camera then snapped some pictures.

I could barely make out Terry, the woman in front of him. She sounded shaken up. I later learned she had flown over the handlebars of her sled, nearly driving off the side of the cliff, while I was off lost in the woods. Luckily the deep snow behaved like a safety net, though she was still a nervous wreck

Barely visible, I could see Terry's silhouette hop off the sled to stretch.

"Do you think they'll be back?" she nervously blared through the blowing snow.

"I hope so," Ron shouted. "This is really intense."

"Tell me about it," I yelled against the wailing wind. "Call me crazy, but my husband and I knew two guys back in Wisconsin who knew everything there was to know about snowmobiles. They are both deceased now, but they've been with me this entire time. They keep telling me that everything will be okay."

"That's reassuring," Ron replied. "Right now we could use all the help we can get."

The ridge was so rocky with so much steep, we all had to file one-by-one down the side of the mountain. A grueling and chilly hour passed before we were all finally rescued.

Since my snowmobile was the heaviest of the bunch (the leads had nicknamed it the Cadillac), the only safe way to guide me down was to have me move to the passenger seat while one of the leads took control of my sled. "Lean to the far left," he warned, "This will be steep, so hang on!" I then watched him plant his feet firmly on the left floorboard and shift all of his weight to the side to prevent us from tipping over the edge.

I held my breath and clung to the safety bars.

The ride down was so nerve-racking and bumpy that at one point my helmet slammed into his back.

"We're with you," Corey reassured me.

"Just enjoy the experience" Tom joked.

I couldn't help but smile.

I finally made it to the ground. Thank you God, and thank you Corey and Tom!

Not only did the entire ordeal bond me more closely to everyone, but I now finally understand why true passion is said to take your breath away.

ETE = Enjoy the Experience™
Lesson learned Feb 9, (year 2)

PERCEPTION IS EVERYTHING

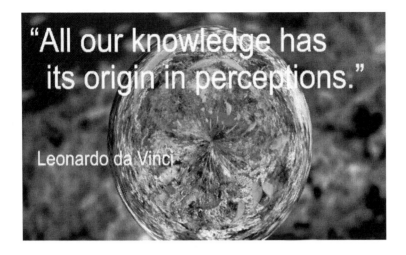

"All our knowledge has its origin in perceptions."

Leonardo da Vinci

What a phenomenal lunar eclipse we experienced this week! The full moon lit up the sky, completely disappeared and then fully re-appeared. It was amazing to watch!

My sister, Squirt, sent me an email a couple of days later explaining that a lunar eclipse is a full moon "supercharged." When the moon's reflection gets blocked, we're left in the dark. When we no longer see the light, our viewpoints get twisted.

Perhaps this is why people say "perception is everything."

Perception is defined as "cognition, understanding and immediate or intuitive recognition or appreciation."
To perceive is "to become aware of ; to know."
(Webster's)

WORDS FOR THE SOUL

How often do you have a twisted view of your Self?

When you aren't operating in the light, you're in a false perception, full of shadows, fears, and doubts.

This came into realization last night when I went night skiing with a couple of girlfriends.

"I'm not really good yet," I explained. "This is only my second season skiing in the mountains."

"Neither are we," they laughed. "But, we'll have a lot of fun."

The sun sat low in the bright blue sky as we headed up the lift. Shadows from the trees moved in unison as the high speed chairs swept us up the mountain and onto the ridge.

We took off down a run, and I quickly learned just how inexperienced I was compared to them.

After just one intermediate run, I was already huffing and puffing, and they were barely winded.

"Let's do this one while we still have some sun," said one friend pointing toward a more advanced trail.

"Sounds good," the other said. Then she flew down the mountain in perfect formation.

My other friend followed, as my legs began to shake.

"Be careful. It's pretty icy," she called out from ahead. "The shadows have set in."

(They had indeed)

I could see her light blue jacket whizzing down the slope.

The run was slalom, so it was much narrower than most of the runs I have done, and though I had gone skiing the whole day before, I hadn't worked my way up to this level yet.

My heart began to race.

This was my first time out with these girls, so my ego wanted to look good, yet how was I going to do this without making a complete fool of myself?

"I can do this," I told myself. "I WILL get down safely."

I slowly began to traverse the mountainside, but the snow was really crusted. I could barely keep an edge.

Moments later, down I went.

Picture this . . . One pole was lying vertically above my head, the other far off to my right. Both of my skis had miraculously popped off near my feet. From an eagle's point of view I would have looked like a flailed arms and legs snow splat.

Though I was embarrassed and nervous, I mustered up enough strength to pull myself up the mountain to retrieve my first pole.

Then I slowly turned my body to grab my skis and second pole.

I was so far up the mountain I could barely make out my friends who were standing at the base patiently waiting for me.

This only made me more nervous. I had wished they weren't watching. I felt so silly really.

Deep down I knew I shouldn't be embarrassed. I have only had two ski lessons, and compared to their 15+ years of skiing, I was still so new at this.

Oh no! Vertigo was setting in.

I started to feel really dizzy.

Stop looking at the drop off! Focus on your footing, I told myself.

There was no way I'd be able to pop my skis back on at this angle. I was just too inexperienced for the steepness at this point.

Carefully, I lifted my skis and my poles to start my icy trek down the cliff. I carefully dug the heels of each boot into the heavy packed snow with each and every step, positioning my skis and poles off to the side so as not to slip and fall. As you might imagine, I felt like a mountain goat without any hooves.

Each step I took was cautious and deliberate.

Finally, when I was close enough, I called out to my friends.

"Please go on without me," I yelled.

"Never," they shouted. "We're in this with you."

"Please," I nearly begged. "This is embarrassing."

"Okay," they gave in, "We'll do another run and meet you at the bottom."

From the looks of it, I still had at least 500 yards to move.

My entire body was full of sweat, and my muscles were really weak.

As soon as I felt it was safe, I inched over to the side of the slope and fully collapsed in the cold snow.

I was just so very tired. I needed to rest for a while.

Several yards ahead of me, an older gentleman lost his footing and took a digger too.

"Rome wasn't build in a day," his friend yelled as she raced down past him.

Determined, the man who fell spent several minutes struggling in hopes he could punch his skis back on.

After several minutes, he gave up.

Clearly exhausted, he then grabbed his skis and poles and started sliding down the mountain on his rump.

"Looks like we're in the same boat," he yelled as he slid down the slope.

I began to laugh.

We were definitely a sight to see, yet how wonderful it was to not be in this alone.

Watching this man try to lift himself up with such determination somehow helped me work up enough courage to want to try again too, so after a few more deep breaths I made another attempt to punch on my skis.

And would you believe that after just a little effort, I WAS able to do it!

Whoo-Hoo!

Though I was pretty nervous about the whole thing and my muscles felt like jelly, I finally was able to ski back down safely to the base.

And, yes, by the time I reached the ground, my expert-skier friends had already gotten back from their second run.

(You can stop laughing now. - hee-hee)

"Please go on without me," I pleaded to my friends. "My entire body feels like an over-stretched rubber-band."

"Are you sure?" they questioned.

"I insist," I said.

Off they went like two foxy bunnies in the snow. Obviously I was jealous. "If only I were half as good as them," I said to myself in a sigh.

After 30 minutes of rest, I finally chose an easy green run to regain my confidence.

Half way through, however, my muscles began to burn so bad I had wished I hadn't pushed myself to ski two days in a row.

Stop here

It was God directing me to rest awhile more. I was happy to comply.

I pushed down the tips of my poles into the binds of my skis to release my boots. Then, I sat back into a drift and planted my bottom firmly in the snow.

The coolness of mother's nature's ice-pack felt really good on my legs.

I closed my eyes and began to go within.

Suddenly a rush of messages freely flowed . . .

Perceive your Self as someone who frees her self from the paralyzation of fear.

Perceive your Self as someone who can face humiliation.

Perceive your Self as someone who will no longer remain paralyzed in fear.

Perceive your Self as someone who is finally living in the Light.

I began to smile and then opened my eyes.

There out in the distance was the most spectacular view of the setting sun. Its loving warm orange and yellow rays of energy filled my entire essence with patience and love, giving me a whole wonderful new perception of ME!

ETE = Enjoy the Experience™
Lesson learned on Feb 23, (year 2)

ROSE TO THE OCCASION

"But friendship is the breathing rose, with sweets in every fold."

~ Oliver Wendell Holmes

Winter has snapped coldly once again. Our freshly mowed lawn is covered in powder and the grey clouds are persistent with no signs of the sun.

A colleague of mine from the college was commenting about her mountain estate still fully buried in two feet of snow.

"It's depressing," she said with a frown.

Then, just as I was about to empathize, she fully recovered with a smile, "But, I'm learning to accept it for the good. This snow will help keep forest fires down."

I began smiling too. What a wonderful new outlook she had!

Her quick wit allowed her to catch her negative comments and quickly turn them around.

Yet, sometimes it's not that easy, is it? Sometimes we can be so stuck in negativity that we're unable to pull ourselves back up without some loving help from a friend.

Greek philosopher, Epictetus believed all human beings have the freedom to control their lives and to live in harmony with nature.

He said, "The key is to keep company only with people who uplift you, whose presence calls forth your best."

Uplift means to "to raise; elevate" and "to exalt emotionally or spiritually." (Webster's)

Looking back on my life, I could have used Epictetus' advice a little sooner. In grade school I chose a "best friend" who liked to slug my arm and leave a bruise.

In junior high, I "befriended" two girls who were into drinking, drugs, and shoplifting, and when I didn't give in to their peer-pressure-some-ways my face and eyes became their punching bags.

Things got so bad, in fact, that by the time high school arrived, I began planning my own suicide.

If only I had known then I was an intuitive empath, it would have made much more sense why I was melding myself with everyone around me and unable to decipher my own Self.

I recall being in study hall and looking through my notebook at all my written goodbye notes and wondering if anyone would even miss me.

Through my sad eyes, I looked up briefly and saw a classmate named Tyrelle come into the room and hand a"pink slip"to the study hall teacher.

Imagine my surprise, when my name was called aloud.

I was a straight A student. What in the world had I done wrong?

I could barely walk down the hall to the guidance counselor's office I was such a bundle of nerves.

"How are you today?" Mr. Mommaerts inquired through his '80's style wide framed glasses.

Big tears pooled in my eyes like a sudden tidal wave.

"Your friend, Tyrelle, tells me you've been showing signs of depression. Would you care to talk about it?"

My mind began to scramble. Tyrelle? The girl who brought in the note? She considered me a friend? How could this be? She's popular and outgoing and nice.

"Tyrelle tells me you've been more sad than usual. What's going on in your life?"

- How did she know this?
- What gave it away?
- Was there really someone out there who noticed my pain?

Was it truly possible that Tyrelle cared about me, and not because I was someone's daughter or sister or cousin or grandchild, but because Tyrelle had noticed me as I really am???

Yes indeed. Tyrelle and I became genuine friends after that day, and she never lost her ability to read me like a book.

Whenever times were tough, she would present me with a red rose, and throughout the years I would do the same for her. When we broke up with a boyfriend, out came the tissues and a single red rose.

If one of us was feeling distant and down, it was time for a pep talk and a long stemmed rose.

I honestly believe Tyrelle was sent here from Heaven to help me stay uplifted, alive, and authentically whole. Why?

Because before that day in the guidance counselor's office, I never really understood what it meant to have a true friend.

Heck! Until I met Tyrelle I never knew how to be one.

Sadly, I was forced to present my last rose to Ty in her casket just a few years ago. A tragic car accident took her young life on a cold wintery night.

Today, as I walk to my mailbox and gaze at the snow, I am in a melancholy mood. How can I change my dismal outlook so the clouds aren't so full of gloom?

As I reach for the bundle of letters, I have my answer . . .

Ty's 13 year-old daughter is writing me from the Midwest. Reminiscent tears stream onto the page as I open picture after picture of the most uplifting photos of the rose!!

I miss you and love you, too, Tyrelle... my genuine and beautiful friend!

"True love cannot be seen by the eyes, but only felt by the spirit."

Michelle Skaletski-Boyd The Corporate Woo-Woo™

ETE = Enjoy the Experience™
Lesson learned April 19, (year 2)

IMAGINATION...CARRIED AWAY

"When you get ahead of your Self,
Remember to always detach and let go."

Michelle Skaletski-Boyd The Corporate Woo-Woo™

Life threw us a curve ball, and all I knew to do was to lie down and cry.

Steve and I were told by the adoption agency this week that Cynthia is to remain with her birth parent now, per a ruling by the Attorney General's office.

When I first heard the news I could feel my heart cracking as it tumbled into millions of shattered pieces full of "why me's" and "what if's."

Sadness immediately consumed me as my once shining internal sun fell sullenly behind its horizon.

My journal became my escape, allowing me to dive head-first into every page as I cried, and I sulked, and I questioned my faith. My cycle of depression lasted for days.

The breaking point came when I headed to the city for an appointment with a woman named, Debbie, who is a licensed esthetician.

I was scheduled to see her for a brow shaping treatment, but what I received was so much more.

Debbie and I have talked about adoption many times. She, herself, was adopted when she was only 5-1/2 years old, so she was naturally curious to know how things had been progressing since our last appointment.

"What's new with that little girl?" she asked as she applied hot wax to the ridge above my eye.

I choked up and explained the situation, unable to hold back my tears. "I'm sorry," I confessed, "You're the first person I've talked to about this, other than Steve."

"It's okay," Debbie reassured.

"I've never been pregnant before," I said, "but it feels like I miscarried somehow, and I feel so silly really. I painted her room, told all my family and friends, and even went out and bought her some gifts."

Debbie lovingly put her hand on mine.

"Never buy gifts until after the child moves in with you," she advised, "but, now that you have, make sure the gifts go to her since they were meant for her."

"Okay," I agreed.

Debbie went on to say that women in particular dream of fairy tale endings, but when it comes to adoption, the real test is whether or not there's true love.

"What do you mean?" I asked.

"Do you remember the feeling you had when you first met your husband?" she inquired.

"Yes," I replied, smiling for the first time that day.

"Did you have that same love-at-first-sight feeling with this little girl?"

I thought for a moment and then truthfully admitted, "No."

"If and when it's meant to be, you will," she insisted.

"I got it with my adopted parents, and they got it with me. Without it, you're just feeling sorry for the child or falling in love with the idea. Either way, it's not the same. Because having those strong magical feelings upfront is what gets you through the tough times no matter what."

Debbie was right. How could I have forgotten my own advice? I had taken a leap of faith but had not found the true signs and symbols to show me for sure that this was "it."

So after my session with Debbie, I went for a walk with Buddy to clear my head.

It was lightly raining, and the sweet fragrance of the lilac trees filled my entire being as I began meditation.

Why has this happened, God?

He gently whispered . . .

You allowed your imagination to get carried away.

I was confused by this, because I had heard imagination was a key to building intuition, so I had to look up the word to understand.

Imagination is "the act or power of forming a mental image of something not present to the senses"; "fanciful or empty assumption." (Webster's)

A-Ha! My imagination got carried away because I jumped at the first opportunity that came along without receiving a strong internal knowing.

It was just like going to the Junior Girls' prom knowing full well my date was not for me. Yet, I so desperately wanted someone to take that I got swept up in the idea and was willing to settle for less.

This event was similar. Steve and I had good intentions yet got hung up in the fairytale without really feeling the spiritual pull. ~ Another lesson learned.

ETE = Enjoy the Experience™
Lesson learned June 7, (year 2)

SECRETS TO SELF-ACCEPTANCE

"Self-acceptance comes from meeting
Life's challenges vigorously.
Don't numb yourself to your trials and difficulties
nor build mental walls to exclude pain from your life.
You will find peace not by trying to escape
Your problems but by confronting them."

~ Yogi, Swami Kriyananda

Another week has quickly passed. The weather has remained uncertain - as if spring is reluctant to come out and play.

Steve and I have had the pleasure of hosting his parents this week.

They have generously given of themselves in many ways, from laughter and hugs, to helping out with daily cleaning and evening meals.

Their presence has been exactly the ray of sunshine that Steve and I have needed most. (Thanks Mom and Dad B.!)

Having Steve's parents here has helped me reveal my "lesson of the week," and for those of you who aren't quite certain what this means, I'll take a moment to explain. Over the last couple of years, I've been fortunate enough to have lessons of life present themselves to me, and I have intuitively began to recognize that it's my mission to openly and humbly share these lessons with you.

It's sort of like receiving clue-after-clue from the Universe and then tuning in to God to achieve a higher understanding of what it means.

This past week, for example, I continued to receive thematic messages that centered around people who were hoping to conceal something about themselves that was causing them not to stand fully in their truth.

One friend was afraid to admit she has never planned a big event before, yet once she pushed past her fear, many individuals stepped forward to help.

Another friend was debating whether or not she should use a new Vet for her pet. She was afraid that if she did, she'd have to explain herself to the former one.

I politely suggested this may be the Universe's way of telling her she just may need to be more assertive. After all, the world often reflects back to us the things we need to face in order to finally move forward.

And, just yesterday morning, Steve's parents and I had a conversation that was similar.

We were relating with one another about how sometimes we want others to think we're doing better than we really are, because we're afraid to admit we could use some extra help or because we've become fearful of what others might think.

Yet, is it true that what we fear we always draw more near?

I know that unless we come to terms with our fears we'll continue to be reminded of their presence in all types of scary shapes and forms.

And so it goes, these were my clues for the week.

I filed them carefully in my memory bank and then.

meditated awhile to ask God what they're intended to mean.

I was sitting in an open field with Buddy. We had gone there to play ball, and after several rounds of fetch, his furry body got tired and he began chewing on a stick.

I closed my eyes and began focusing on my breathing. I became fully aware of the flat cool stone beneath my bottom, the chirping of the birds in the trees, and the light blowing wind gently caressing my face.

I consciously reached in my mind for each awaiting clue for it seemed fear was a common theme, but why?

- What is it that prevents us from speaking the truth?
- Why do we sometimes hide from the world and pretend that everything's okay?
- How come we often feel like it's better to put on a happy face than to admit we are hurting or need help?

I placed my thumbs and middle fingers together then turned my palms to face the sky.

Breathing deeply, I envisioned my body grounded to the earth with a strong stream of energy flowing freely through me, from my tailbone to my head.

White light permeated around me as God's calm words resonated within.

Open your eyes

I saw a field of straw-like grass protruding from the ground with a few green weeds scattered in-between.

?

- Do you think the grass cares what the weed thinks?
- Does the weed hide the fact that it's a weed?
- Does either pretend they're doing well even when they're not?

I couldn't help but giggle.
Immediately, I knew what each clue meant.

Self is "a person's nature or character."

To accept means "to take or receive" and "to regard as true or sound." (Webster's)

When we are openly receptive to our natural character, we come to accept our Self.

In other words, 'how' we thrive is dependent on our admissions of the truth.

Admitting our reasons for the choices that we make or the blemishes that we bear will often come with a lot of resistance.

Why?

Because our egos don't like to give up control or admit we have weaknesses and faults. We fear we may be rejected or not liked. It's an ultimate test of our being and helps explain why we sometimes hide from the truth by saying we shouldn't have to explain our actions or justify our decisions to 'anyone about anything at any time'.

Yet, just as the grass comes with its weeds, we, too, have foibles and faults.

Personal growth can only flourish when we fully accept our Self — flaws and all.

The acceptance of Self has no tolerance for measuring and no room for fears, so take time every day to stand in front of a mirror and loudly and positively declare ... (Fill in the 'blank' for your Self.) - "Despite my own fear of (BLANK), I wholly and completely accept my Self."

Complete Self-acceptance means knowingly appreciating, validating, and supporting everything about your Self exactly as it is, in-the-here-and-the-now.

Self-acceptance is admitting to trusted friends that you're hurting so they can help you heal; it's tactfully disclosing your preferences so all involved may move forward on the spiritual path; and it's revealing your weaknesses to confidants so that stronger talents can have the room to emerge.

So, go ahead, accept your Self. You'll feel so much better when you do!

ETE = Enjoy the Experience™
Lesson learned Apr 5, (year 2)

COMMITTED

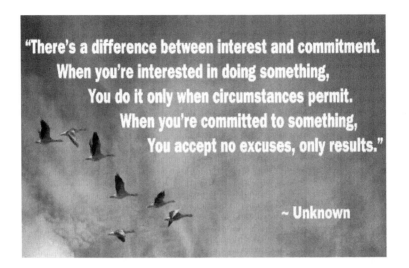

"There's a difference between interest and commitment.
When you're interested in doing something,
You do it only when circumstances permit.
When you're committed to something,
You accept no excuses, only results."

~ Unknown

**Commit means "to give in trust;" "to pledge or
engage oneself." (Webster's)**

I hadn't realized the importance of commitment until I was meditating recently near the fast flowing river.

Record snowfalls combined with sunny temps have caused the river to roar. The once clear blue waters have now turned to roily, restless whitecaps.

My eyes were fixated on the steady rhythmic beating of each wave as I fell deeper and deeper into a subconscious state.

It's been over a year since I announced my desire to write my first book.

Though I have a strong passion to make a positive difference in this world, lack of commitment on my part is causing my battery to drain.

It's time for a serious jumpstart.

God diverted my attention from the current and over to the river's edge.

My eyes fell upon a floating limb caught in a sluggish eddy.

It was aimlessly drifting between two fallen trees.

You are like the limb, clinging with little result. Be like the water. Trust the steady flow.

God was right! My opportunity to write is now.

Gone are the days of excuses and exceptions.

With progression comes commitment, and with commitment comes possible risk.

I realize now that I'm sitting at a fork in the bend.

Once I jump in, there will be no turning back. I will be leaving my present comfort zone and heading in a new direction.

I can already feel the change.

Not only will I focus more on creating my book, but I'll also give more attention to bringing a child into my life.

Yes. Steve and I were contacted by a state social worker last week telling us we've been matched with a six year old girl.

For reasons of confidentiality, we'll call this little girl, Cynthia.

And, though it's not official yet, my husband and I are being asked to commit ourselves to foster care parenting with the intention to adopt.

I'm ecstatic and afraid and in shock.

Everything's happening so fast, and the scariest thing is that at any given moment Cynthia could be reunited with her birth parent.

My fears have pulled me toward clinging to safety, yet instinct tells me it's time to take the plunge.

Though it may be weeks yet before Cynthia moves into our home, Steve and I got the chance to meet with her earlier in the week.

She was like a little light that lit up the room with a tiny small giggle attached.

After playing a game of Candy Land, Cynthia turned toward Steve and said, "You want me to come live with you, don't you?"

Steve's smile burst wide open.

"What did you say?" he grinned.

"Oh, nothing," she retracted with a snicker. Then, she buried her face in her hands.

"Do you want to come live with us?" Steve quizzed.

"Yes." she giggled.

"Are you sure?" I teased. "We have lots and lots of rules."

"I can follow rules." she pleaded. "I can make my bed and pick up my toys. . ." (the list went on and on)

"Okay," I said. "But there's one really important rule that is the grandest rule of all."

"What is it?" Cynthia shrieked. "Tell me. Tell me please."

"You have to give really good hugs."

Cynthia's eyes filled with glee. "Really strong ones?" she screeched.

"Yep," I smiled.

It was as though Cynthia's feet couldn't move fast enough.

Her strawberry shortcake body darted right into my lap as she wrapped her loving arms tightly around my neck.

I was barely able to hold back the tears.

Though I had promised myself I'd remain guarded so as not to get hurt, at that very moment, my heart melted.

There was no going back.
It's now a leap of faith.

ETE = Enjoy the Experience™
Lesson learned May 31, (year 2)

A TIME OF RECREATION

"TO THINE OWN SELF BE TRUE"
William Shakespeare

It's officially summer, and what an exciting week it's been! Not only was I involved in another great inspirational speaking event, but I also was a guest for an online radio show and had an absolute blast!

The host helped me fully realize that I am indeed at my happiest when I'm spreading seeds of "life lessons" throughout the world.

When we spend time doing the things we love to do, everything else will naturally fall into place.

So how do you know what you truly love to do?

Begin by closing your eyes and inviting your inner child to come out and play.

Yes. You read correctly. Play. Just like you did as a kid!!

When you engage in play it awakens your creative side, the connection to your spiritual Self. And since your spiritual Self craves recognition, why not give it what it needs?

All it takes is a little bit of child's play.

During many of my inspirational events, I bring along a big bucket of toys. I love to watch my audience's inner child come alive as the entire room begins to spin jacks, toss squish balls and hike plastic fish into the air.

It's really so much fun!! When we engage in fun, we are literally re-creating ourselves. That's why we call it recreation.

Recreation is defined as "a pastime and a diversion affording relaxation and enjoyment." (Webster's)

Allow your Self to kick off your shoes walk around the house or run through the blades of grass; Play in the tub by flapping your arms and pretending you're a duck; Run though a sprinkler and laugh; Climb a tree; Play a game of kick ball; Color in a coloring book; Blow some bubbles; or Drink some juice from a curly straw, and feel like you're a kid again.

There's fun all around just waiting for you to enjoy.

Take my walk with Buddy earlier in the week. We came upon a sidewalk full of a child's chalk drawings. For those of you who remember, it was like walking into my very own version of "Hello my name is Simon."

First there was a smiling happy face drawn in the prettiest of pink chalks. If it could talk it would have said "Life is great!"

Then there was a bright yellow sun glowing for the world to see.

Next was a flower filled with brilliant pastel colors of purple, pinks and blues.

At the very end was a beautiful artistic rendition of a hopscotch game. – I couldn't help but try it out.

"Hold on a minute Bud," I said, as I bent down to tie my tennis shoe laces tight.

He watched as I then picked up a stone and tossed it into the first square.

Smiling, I hopped over square one and into square two and then onto three. Both feet landed firmly into squares four and five.

I hopped, hopped, hopped and turned around and then hopped back into square two and bent down to pick up my stone marker from square one as I laughed like a little kid again.

I found my inner child!

Hop, Hop, Hop, jump and land on both feet! Hop, Hop, Hop. Boy that sure was neat!!!

ETE = Enjoy the Experience™
Lesson learned June 23, (year 1)

MIRRORING REFLECTION

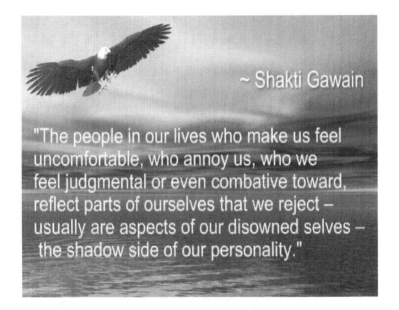

~ Shakti Gawain

"The people in our lives who make us feel uncomfortable, who annoy us, who we feel judgmental or even combative toward, reflect parts of ourselves that we reject – usually are aspects of our disowned selves – the shadow side of our personality."

This past Sunday, Steve and I took Buddy out on the canoe. It was our first venture "paddle" since last September.

As we gently floated across the crystal clear lake, a beautiful bald eagle spread its wings and soared peacefully from treetop to shore.

We watched as it gathered food and then flew peacefully back toward the clouds. Its beautiful black and white toned body glided freely toward the treetops as our eyesight adjusted to the light.

"Look at the nest," I loudly whispered as I carefully turned back toward Steve. He returned my smile with a nod.

We both pulled up our paddles and allowed the canoe to drift free.

The amazing eagle once again emerged from the crown of the trees and flew to a nearby branch.

My eyes fixated on its nest as a dark brown mottled head poked up from its circular twigged retreat just as its long flight feathered wings began to flap furiously.

It was as if I was watching a scene from *National Geographic*. It was an amazing experience by far.

This baby eaglet must have been at least six weeks old because it was nearly as big as its mom.

Hearing it screech reminded me of the story about a farmer who was walking across his land just after a windy storm when he discovered an eagle's egg lying in the grass.

The farmer gently lifted the warm egg to his hands then carefully carried it to the barn where he placed it beneath a setting hen.

A few days later, a little eaglet hatched.

Having been raised by the hen, this little eaglet mimicked the chicks by pecking about the farmyard and rarely looking up.

One day though, the little eaglet was out scrambling for feed when Father Eagle flew by. He noticed his baby eaglet, quickly circled back and gave out a very loud screech.

"What are you doing down there?" Father Eagle yelled to his son. "You are not a chicken. You are an eagle. Eagles are not made to live in a barnyard. Eagles are meant to fly. The heavens are your domain. Come up here with me."

The little eaglet was very scared. He believed he was a chicken after all.

Father Eagle urged him to jump up and flap his wings. "You can fly if you try," he encouraged.

So, the little eaglet gave it his all, flapping his wings so hard he landed just outside of the coop.

Father Eagle screeched with excitement. "You can do it. Jump higher, Son. Spread your wings to fly."

It was a silver dollar!

The little eaglet did what father said, and by a mighty jump of faith stretched his mighty wings and soared.

I love this story, because all creatures of this world are optical images of our being.

Sometimes you see only fears; other times you're reminded you can fly.

A mirror is "a reflecting surface; something that gives a minutely faithful representation, image or idea of something else." (Webster's)

Who are the people in your life?
What parts of you do they mirror?

ETE = Enjoy the Experience™
Lesson learned July 12, (year 2)

A PART WITH MY SELF

"We cannot become what we need to be
By remaining what we are."
~ Max DePree

So much has happened since we've moved from Wisconsin. I have to keep convincing myself that it's been nearly a year since I resigned from the phone company to pursue my dreams!

My biography is now appearing alongside some wonderful gurus, and I have to keep pinching myself because I keep on thinking this isn't real.

In fact I was telling a friend the other day that I feel like I'm driving through life right now with one foot on the gas and one foot on the brake.

Though I'm very excited to be moving in such a positive direction, it's a brand new experience for me, so I abruptly halt and then find myself going into a tailspin.

Like last week when I knew my first video would be debuting for the world to see. Though I had been guided to do it, self-doubt kept creeping in.

My husband Steve could see what was happening, but there was really nothing he could do other than to be patient and keep reassuring me that everything would be okay once I took my foot off the brake.

I kept second-guessing everything . . .

?

- Did I make the right decision?
- Did I choose the right topic?
- Would my new video be welcomed by the world?

It was a classic case of Self-sabotage.

Self-sabotage is deliberating putting up obstacles in front of your Self to avoid possible disappointment along your life's path to purpose.

It's completely fear based and full of personal disruption.

Disruption is "forcible separation or division into parts." (Webster's)

In other words, you forget that you're part of the whole.

You begin to feel smaller than you really are, you start to wonder if you really have what it takes, you begin to see flaws where there are none, and you cycle through cobwebs of fear.

In fact, disruption caused by Self-sabotage brings chaos into your life.

So ask your Self, is it time to get out of your own way?
Is it time to bravely step aside?

ETE = Enjoy the Experience™
Lesson learned Nov 3, (year 1)

CREATING SPIRITUAL SPACE

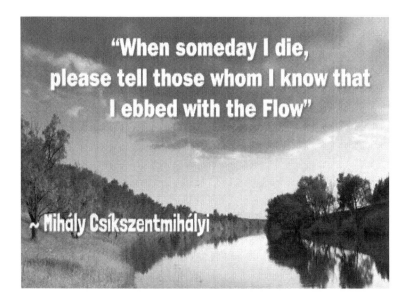

"When someday I die, please tell those whom I know that I ebbed with the Flow"

~ Mihály Csikszentmihályi

Earlier this week my younger sister and brother flew in for a visit.

It's been enjoyable watching them experience the mountains for the first time – from the fresh falling summit snow, to the vibrant fall painted trees, to the beautiful fast flowing river.

When my siblings first arrived, we were ecstatic to see each other, yet deep down we were all wondering, 'Would we get along?'

It had been 15+ years since we shared the same roof, and though we all had the best of intentions no one knew for sure just how long it would last.

Just a few minutes after leaving the airport, I made a few "unexpected" pit stops. This threw my sister off since she was planning on going straight to her new room to drop off her luggage. When she found out we were instead stopping off at the grocery store she grew a little perturbed.

My brother lovingly nudged her.

"Just go with the flow," he said.

Little did I know just how much this piece of advice would come in handy.

Just an hour into the visit, as my sister and brother were unpacking their luggage, I quickly learned that making room for their stay would be more than just emptying closets and drawers.

I had overlooked the concept of making room for spiritual space, and because of this I was about to learn a very valuable lesson about what it really means to "go with the flow."

Space is defined as "the unlimited great 3-dimensional realm in which all material objects are located and all events occur." (Webster's)

When we look at "going with the flow" from a scientific perspective, we learn matter is made up of condensed energy and energy is a big bundle of power.

Spiritually speaking, energy needs to be positive for spiritual space to occur.

Spiritual space is a dimension that goes beyond the physical world; it's an intangible power that dances positively to and fro as long as there's room for it to move.

Spiritual space can't be touched physically, but it can be 'felt' intuitively. When it's used in a loving way it is sensing other's emotions and knowing those around you are supporting you positively even when no words are spoken.

I'd be fibbing if I told you I was able to create spiritual space that very first night. In fact, I was a bit displaced.

I found myself wondering if the guest rooms were comfortable enough or if the common household routines would be accepted or rejected. These worries were constricting the space.

And, because I wanted to control the cosmic waves of the room, the spiritual energies began clogging up, and everyone present could 'feel' it.

By the next morning, both my siblings reported getting a poor night's rest, and I could start to feel my Self spin.

I needed to meditate with my Maker . . .

After a few deep breaths God showed me a scene of my acupuncturist's office. I was lying on the table receiving a treatment for infertility. As the doctor gently inserted the needles, he explained how the meridians and energy flows . . .

According to Chinese medicine, he said, good health is a stream of positive energy moving freely to all meridians in the body. When this positive energy is disturbed, it will negatively affect the flow.

During this memory and right on cue, God broke in . . .

The same goes for spiritual space. To keep the energy positive, you must go with the flow.

I inhaled deeply and opened my eyes.

A-Ha! Going with the flow doesn't mean conforming. It means allowing.

From a fuzzy bumblebee flying indoors to an out-of-town guest or a new child in your home, you are only capable of exchanging positive energy with every living being when you allow things to remain in the space of spiritual flow.

Otherwise, tension and resistance builds and positive energy stops flowing freely, and then negative energy takes form.

Having my sister and my brother here for a visit has really opened my eyes. I'm now able to see the importance of going with the flow in this glorious field of spiritual space.

ETE = Enjoy the Experience™
Lesson learned Sept 29, (year 1)

DESTINATION UNKNOWN

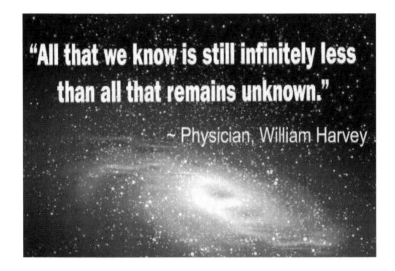

"All that we know is still infinitely less than all that remains unknown."

~ Physician, William Harvey

The weekend forecast predicts bright sunny skies over the next five days.

What a drastic change compared to the recent winter storm advisory that dumped 3 - 10 inches of snow across the mountainous valley.

Imagine the school kids surprise when they woke to a lawn covered in nature's frosted flakes on the first day of their summer vacation.

What a reminder of how unpredictable life can be!

I am definitely learning to be more tolerant of these things. Years ago I would get very upset because things didn't go as planned.

I seriously would calendar all of my dates in permanent ink, which meant there was no room for last minute changes. And back then Steve was a fly-by-the-seat of your pants kind of guy. "Let's just wing it," he'd say.

"Are you kidding?" I'd bellow with my pen behind my ear, one hand on my hip, and the other clutching my calendar. "I need to plan!"

I was completely consumed by the need to be in control. I wish I were exaggerating, but it's true.

It was important I knew everything ahead of time so I could precisely predict what was going on.

In fact, everything I did was calculated with careful consideration at every turn.

I was one of those methodical people who needed to know exactly where we'd be sleeping and where we'd be eating on every given road trip and every vacation destination.

"Who cares!" Steve would say. "We'll sleep in the car if we need to, and our bodies can go for days without food."

I remember getting so mad. Nearly 17 years later and the tables have turned.

Steve is now the one who "needs to know."

Imagine my amusement this past Wednesday just before dinner when Steve asked, "Do you want to go to our land or take a motorcycle trip this Sunday?"

"Let's just play it by ear," I smiled.

His face became very serious then.

"Well, Michelle, I'd like to plan," he declared.

My cackle could be heard for miles.

I "busted a gut" you might say.

Never in a million years did I think Steve would be the planner and I'd be the spur-of-the-moment one in the relationship.

Our friend Susan, a certified counselor, says there are stages throughout any relationship in which roles flip and turn so that balance can be maintained as both individuals transform. "You're the true 'Yin and the Yang,'" she said.

How beautiful is that!

It's also helped me understand that "Now" appears in the word unknown for a reason.

When we befriend the unknown, we make peace with the present moment.

Unknown means "not within the range of one's understanding."

The "now" has not yet come.

Now means " at the present time or moment." (Webster's)

Right now is the only "IS" there is.

Will we go to the land tomorrow or take a motorcycle trip?

Will it snow again this summer or remain warm and sunny?

Will my book get published or won't it?

Will Steve and I get to be parents or not?

I'm lovingly embracing the unkNOWn, and it feels a lot freer this way.

ETE = Enjoy the Experience™
Lesson learned June 14, (year 2)

IS THE TRUTH MEANT TO HURT?

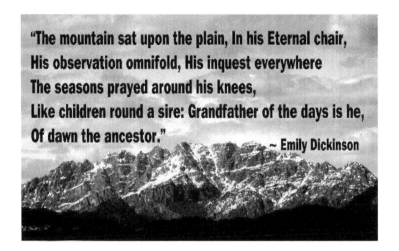

"The mountain sat upon the plain, In his Eternal chair,
His observation omnifold, His inquest everywhere
The seasons prayed around his knees,
Like children round a sire: Grandfather of the days is he,
Of dawn the ancestor."
~ Emily Dickinson

I took my place at the park's picnic table on Friday afternoon when Mother Nature presented a mirror in which I finally looked.

What began as slush-like snow turned into lightly falling rain.

Off to my right, the clouds began to separate just enough for the sun to fully emerge while the rain continued to fall.

I then turned to my left, expecting to see much the same, amazed to find the blue sky pushing away the rain while half of the moon brightly appeared in opposite direction of the sun.

It was as if I were in two different worlds . . .

Blue sky and the moon on my left. Falling rain with the sun on my right.

Neither made much sense at all, yet both were beautiful just the same.

Steve and I too have had a rollercoaster week.

First, my former co-worker Nicole and her husband

announced the birth of their baby boy! (Welcome Aiden Thomas!)

That very same day, a fertility specialist in the area candidly shared with me that, according to statistics, my odds of getting pregnant are now less than 1%. (Ouch.)

One day later we received devastating news that a friend of ours had died. He was only 40 and married just four years. (Connie, we're so very sorry!)

That same afternoon, we received a phone call from our friend Lindsey who happily announced her engagement to Kris. (Congratulations!)

Talk about ups and downs.

Life and death.

Loss and Love.

It's been 7 years in trying to get pregnant.

When the doctor announced that odds were against us, he paused for a moment, apologizing then for being so open and forthright.

"The truth sometimes hurts," he said, "but at least you now know what you're up against."

His words have remained with me all this week.

Does the truth really hurt, and if so, why?

Truth is defined as "the true state of a matter."
True means "real; genuine; authentic. "   (Webster's)

From a spiritual perspective, "true" represents the Divine, and since God has only love to offer, "the truth hurts" feels more like an oxymoron.

So why then, did my new doctor's words cause me so much pain?

As I sat upon that picnic table at the park and watched the seasonal dances, I began to shed some tears.

Just like the weather, I was feeling both saddened and relieved.

Thankfully, the voice of God emerged . . .

Look at the moon;
See the tops of the pines;
Examine the blades of the grass.

I gazed at each a moment.

Tell me what you see.

Answering in my mind..

I see a moon that is stretching upward in hopes of meeting the sun; I see trees that are reaching outward in hopes of receiving more rain; And I see blades of grass that are restless and not yet extended to where they're really wanting to be.

The truth resonated through me . . .

See the moon again with newfound eyes.
Follow the trunk of the tree.
Look closely at the blades of the grass and tell me
what you see.

Blinking away my tears, I did exactly as I was instructed only this time rather than look through all the rain, I saw the light.

Miraculously, the moon appeared to be swimming in the sky just like a felicitous cookie dunked in ice-cold milk.

I inhaled deeply, not yet certain of my lesson.

Then, I carefully scanned the trees.

Each trunk led my vision to its deeply planted roots, letting me know with certainty that satisfaction was clearly present exactly where it stood.

I was in awe.

My eyes then shifted downward to the dormant grass beneath my dangling feet.

Each dewy blade was resting peacefully showing no signs of disappointment or despair.

Instinctively and immediately I knew that my original perceptions of the moon and the treetops and the blades of grass reaching outward were simply mirror messages of my relentless and painful struggle over the last seven long infertile years.

Confirmation followed.

It's time to stop reaching.
This is your truth.
See it for what it is, and you'll no longer feel
any pain.

Tears continued falling and continue to even as I write.

I can now see how similar my emotions have been to the ever-changing weather.

I'm still in transition, trying my best to come to terms with the fact that pregnancy for Steve and me is simply not part of God's plan.

I share this lesson so openly, because the truth hurts, but only because I've resisted it.

And, though I now feel like a chicken that will never lay an egg, I've come to somehow understand that I must stop reaching for what clearly will never be, and to instead focus on another plan.

ETE = Enjoy the Experience™
Lesson learned March 15, (year 2)

TOTALLY WORTH IT!

"Self-worth comes from one thing --
thinking you are worthy."

~ Dr. Wayne Dyer

It's been a beautiful consistent 80+ degrees, and, oh, how I'm loving July! There's always so much to do.

Steve and I are sneaking up to the property tonight to take in a little R&R. It will be good to bond with the land once again.

Things have been crazy busy, but in a very good way.

I just finished another article for a local magazine, continue to partner with like-minded entrepreneurs, and am getting ready to present to a great group of professionals next week.

Yesterday was really fun as well. I presented a 90-minute keynote to a large group of bankers — many of whom traveled a great distance to attend.

The night before the big speech, I was invited to a cocktail party so I could get to know my attendees better.

They were all a wonderful crowd, and the more I chatted, the more I felt at home. That is, until it came time to leave ...

I was saying my round of goodbyes, promising to see everyone in the morning, when a stern looking banker wagged his finger at me and barked.

"You better be good. We paid a lot of money to see you, so you better be worth it."

"Okay," I forcefully smiled as I backed my way out of the room.

As soon as I reached the hotel's foyer, my brain began to uncoil.

?

- What if you're not any good?
- What if you're really not worth it?
- What if all of your practice and rehearsal is still not enough?

Then what? It was my snapping ego, loudly rambling in my ears.

I walked out to the parking lot, inhaled the mountain air and reminded my Self that how I do will be dependent on how I feel.

I put a smile on my face and rehearsed the whole car ride home.

When I walked into the house, Steve sweetly asked, "Are you ready for your big day tomorrow?"

Yes. I'm ready," I enthusiastically replied even though my reluctant ego still echoed meanly in my head.

"I escaped to the family room and curled up in a chair then began to visualize my entire presentation going well from start to finish. It appeased me enough to sleep.

I awoke very early the next day, laid out my clothes, and began to rehearse once again.

Though I felt confident in my abilities and knew my material well, the words, "You better be worth it" lingered in my brain. It was as if someone were hitting a replay button again and again.

I had only a few minutes remaining before it was time to get dressed, so I set my speech aside, walked out onto the patio and began to meditate.

The cool morning breeze helped clear my head and fill me with the Divine.

God, why am I questioning my Self?

My eyes began to flutter just as my answer (a question) was revealed.

Why do you seek out worthiness?

I thought about this a moment, but nothing more came to mind, and I didn't want to be late.

Forty minutes later, I arrived at the hotel, made sure my equipment was working and met the event planner in the hall.

Within minutes I was being introduced. I quickly scanned the crowd. Whew! There was no sign of the man who had challenged me the night before.

I exhaled a sigh of relief and walked to the front of the room.

"Good morning everyone," I announced with a smile and then continued with the talk.

Just a few minutes later, the stern-looking man walked in. He was holding a cup of coffee and seated himself in center aisle. My heart began to race.

And, as synchronicity would have it, I was just beginning to tell a story about a woman named Sara.

"Sara was in the habit of looking outside of herself to define her Self," I remarked.

As soon as these words left my mouth, I knew they were intended for me. If this ever happened to you, then you know how powerful that can be.

Right then and there, I had a big A-Ha! All this while I had been seeking "out" answers rather than allowing my internal worth to shine.

As I glanced across the room, the stern man didn't look so stern anymore. - In fact, he was glowing from within, being an updated reflection of the brand new me.

It was like I had finally recognized a piece of my Self and valued its beauty again.

Once my speech ended, the man approached me with a smile.

"Great job," he beamed.

"Thank you for being here," I said. If he had only known how much I really meant it.

This man was placed in my life for a reason. He was there to remind me that Self-worth is not dependent on anything of the external world.

Self-worth is "the sense of one's own worth as a person"

Worth is defined as "good or important enough to justify."

Having a 'sense' of self-worth means "a mental discernment, realization or recognition." (Webster's)

When we question whether we're worth it or not, we're viewing the world through ego's eyes and will often fall short and not amount to much.

Self-worth comes from authenticity. It cannot be measured in space or time.

So, recognize your Self and embrace your internal being. Because your internal treasure shines!

ETE = Enjoy the Experience™
Lesson learned July 19, (year 2)

FACING TRANSFORMATION

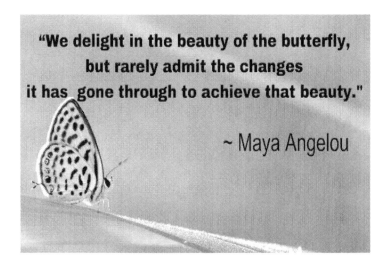

"We delight in the beauty of the butterfly,
but rarely admit the changes
it has gone through to achieve that beauty."

~ Maya Angelou

Just before dinner yesterday the grey sky opened wide and poured buckets of rain so hard and so fast that it sounded like the grand finale of a fireworks show. I kid you not!

Beautiful bolts of July lightning shot across the sky as small gravel-sized hail bounced rapidly off our deck just like an exploding pack of firecrackers.

What a wonderful Independence Day surprise from Mother Nature!

As Steve and I lit our pack of sparklers later that day and waved them high through the air, I said a silent prayer thanking God for my spiritual freedom.

To be independent means "thinking or acting for oneself; not influenced or controlled by others in matters of opinion or conduct; self-confident." (Webster's)

My Self-confidence continues to soar as more business opportunities unfold.

And butterflies are surrounding me this week. A true sign more transition is near.

My maternal Native American upbringing has helped me learn that God's creatures are the medicine for the soul. The butterfly is said to be a symbol of transformation. How very true this is!

The last time I saw a butterfly was just a few weeks before moving to the mountains. I was back on the farm in Wisconsin staring through my upstairs window at the tiny luminescent creature peacefully perched on our rooftop with its uplifted wings to the sky.

It was then I knew it was my time to fly.

Now, a year and a half later, just like a butterfly, I've had to learn to trust in this transition.

Though I'm getting much better than I've ever been before, seeing so many butterflies this week has caused me to wonder, "What's around the corner?"

Hopefully I'll be able to experience it from a place of all that the butterfly represents: freedom, beauty and wonderful changes for the better!

ETE = Enjoy the Experience™
Lesson learned July 5, (year 2)

A GROWTH SPURT

"Life isn't about finding your Self. Life is about Creating Your Self."

~ George Bernard Shaw

After 15 days of working, I finally took a day off this week.

It was truly time.

I was starting to feel unloved, unappreciated and unnoticed.

The more I craved love, the more I withered.

The more I hoped to be seen, the more I disappeared.

The more I sought attention, the more neglected I became.

It wasn't until after a walk through my yard that I began to understand what was happening.

The fresh mulch in the blueberry plants were renewing their growth.

The pruning of the shrubs was bringing out their green . . . Yes, things were in transition, but only because they had been helped along the way.

As I walked over to the rose bush, I noticed new buds were trying to push through the withering flowers of last season. Deadheading would definitely help.

I began plucking each dried blossom.

It was then I realized how much I have been neglecting myself.

Neglect means "paying little or no attention to"   (Webster's)

I had been spending so much time focusing on my business, the resort, the yard and the house that I'd completely forgotten about my Self.

So, today I chose to take the day off, and I went on an enjoyable walk, then I danced around the house to fun music, and then rented a funny movie, and best of all, I got to spend a good portion of the day with my spouse.

It was exactly what I needed!!

God is a wonderful boss!

ETE = Enjoy the Experience™
Lesson learned June 16, (year 1)

CHOOSING THE PATH OF DISCERNMENT

"Discernment is learning to listen to and trust your natural knowing."

~ Author, S. Ryals

Steve and I had an awesome weekend. The weather couldn't have been more beautiful . . . a consistent 78 degrees with a soft light breeze. Riding our Gold Wing through Montana and Wyoming was a wonderful way to spend my birthday this year!

Steve especially enjoyed hopping back into the saddle after working so many hours. It was uplifting to see him so happy again.

This was our second year participating in the Montana Ride for Hope. This wonderful benefit extends itself in more ways than one, not only for the critically ill children who are so appreciative to receive but also for the riders and contributors who are so grateful to give.

Attending this over my birthday felt right.

One rider in particular held a special place in my heart. I couldn't help but notice her as Steve and I were nearing the end of the buffet line.

Her rider pins indicated she had been riding for hope for the last six years.

Just as this woman reached the end of the line, she leaned toward me and said, "There's a reason you and are in line together today. There are no coincidences you know?"

"I believe that is true." I smiled, though it's not every day a complete stranger talks so openly to me.

As fate would have it, by the time Steve and I went through the line the only tables left were with this enlightening woman and her friends.

"I'm Sue," she winked as I sat down. "I told you there was a reason we met."

It turns out Sue is a medical intuitive. She has been gifted with the ability to help others feel good and be healed.

"I can't just tell people what I see," she explained. "Because I need their permission first, but for those who don't ask, I sometimes draw them a map in hopes they'll find their way."

The more Sue and I talked, the more I wanted to ask her what she may have been seeing in me, yet the timing was off, or so it seemed.

Unbeknownst to me, Sue was tossing out healing breadcrumbs the entire time we ate.

She spoke about spirituality and healing and goodness and light. She talked about her own personal journey and the healing gifts she has so often shared

The more she spoke, the more her spirit emitted such a positive vibration that I couldn't help but be drawn to her words like a moth is pulled to a flame..

Then, just as my attention was completely hers, she started to nit pick a bit.

Quickly catching herself, she lightly tapped her mouth then extended her hand in the air.

"Don't judge it," she reminded herself aloud, then lovingly continued to speak.

That one act was so visually powerful that it will forever remain with me.

"Don't judge it!"

To judge means "to decide upon critically." (Webster's)

Now, I don't know about you, but my inner-judge tries very hard to pull out its long black robe, pound its make-believe gavel, and sit upon its superior throne. Sometimes it's as if I'm wearing an invisible sign that reads, 'Ego in charge. I am Queen for the day.'

Thankfully being more consciously aware has helped, because I now understand judging is nothing more than allowing my ego to take over the wheel.

Judging is a 'mine is better than yours' mentality. And it's conditioned in many of us.

In fact, one of my favorite things to do as a child was to play the game 'What's wrong with this picture?' and 'Choose the one that doesn't belong'. I was so good at this, I could do it in my sleep. I was a pro at picking out "flaws" in a flash.

The habit of judging became deeply engrained in my brain.

Judgment is an instilled reaction. It's an incessant need to control and to change.

It's seeing things as they are but wanting them to be another way.

Whether directed inward or outward, judgment creates an illusive dividing wall.

It's a feeling of 'I'm right. You're wrong. My path is better than yours.'

There are even times we judge our inner-judge.

Ahhhh!

So, what does a person do?

How can we move through life without judging anymore?

The answer is discernment.

To discern means "to perceive by sight or some other sense; to distinguish mentally." (Webster's)

In other words, discernment is following your true inner-voice rather than allowing your ego to lead.

This is not always easy, I know.

For several years of marriage, I would judge Steve harshly, criticize him cruelly and try my 'superior' best to change him.

My ego couldn't understand why he did the things he'd do.

Self-talk would sound like this . . .

- Why doesn't he love me more?
- Why is he purposely trying to upset me?
- Why can't he change for the better?

In other words, why was he not becoming more like me?

Take his habit of smoking as an example . . .

My inner-judge used to label Steve's tobacco habit as "bad," because I was unable to come to terms with the fact that he was on his own path.

I erroneously believed that having a soul mate meant taking the exact same spiritual journey together which is why I continuously tried to get Steve to change.

I would beg, plead, threaten and throw out so much guilt that I exhausted myself along the way.

And, the more I resisted, the more Steve persisted.

Then one day, I finally realized that no matter what I did, I'd never be able to change Steve.

He is who he is.

Judging him was getting me nowhere. It was like being a spinning hamster caught in a wheel.

Rather than resist, I needed to allow him to be.

After all, who was I to know what's best for him?

Granted, judging can be very reactive, so even to this day, every time Steve lights up, I have to consciously break the pattern of judging by choosing discernment instead.

Discernment is not agreement.

I intuitively know tobacco is not for me.

Rather, discernment means lovingly knowing the difference between my path and the path of someone else, without putting up barriers or blockades between us.

To discern is to follow what feels right, to allow the Higher Self to lead.

In other words, Steve can be Steve completely, while, I'll choose the best path for me.

ETE = Enjoy the Experience™

Lesson learned on Aug 2, (year 2)

(Note: I am happy to say, as of the publishing of this book, my husband is tobacco free.)

THE OBJECT OF MY AFFECTION

"Dogs are not our whole life, but they make our lives whole."
~ Roger Caras

What crazy weather we've had this month.

Yesterday brought chilly snow flurries all morning long, and today's highs are barely reaching 60 degrees.

Though I know I'd feel better if I went out for a walk, not having my walking "Buddy" around has given me many reasons to be lazy.

Yes, our sweet Golden Retriever, Buddy, is out of remission for awhile. The side of his face became very swollen a few weeks back, and his entire right cheek turned strangely deformed - as if bitten by an insect.

Though the swelling went down temporarily, it was stubbornly determined to stay.

I brought Buddy to the Vet two days ago.

Steve and I were told he was suffering from an abscessed tooth. That would certainly explain his sudden raunchy breath, but even more disturbing, we learned that several small growths on his body, called mast cell tumors, were serious enough to be malignant.

Yes, possibly the big "C" word.

This was devastating news.

Buddy is going on 9 years of age and is the smartest dog I've ever known. What I admire most about him is that no matter what kind of mood I'm in, he's always there to wag his tail and love me no matter what.

I can walk with this dog for miles without putting him on a leash; he knows how to heel on command. Buddy's been a wonderful motivator, because he gives me a reason to walk, run, and play ball in the park. I love that he helps keep me energized and young.

And, though sometimes he can be a bit of a mooch (hee-hee), not having him around has created a sudden void in my world...One that I was not ready yet to face.

Though Steve and I have always joked with one another about how both of our pets are "just" a dog and "just" a cat, they are the closest thing to children we have ever come to know.

Therefore, when we learned Buddy would need to have immediate surgery, it naturally only took a moment before Steve and I agreed he was definitely worth footing the hefty medical bill.

What is it about our pets that cause us to open our wallets and spend more on them than we do on ourselves?

For me, it's Buddy's enormous capacity to offer such unselfish loyalty and benevolent affection no matter what. His intuitive gifts are remarkable. He has this profound ability to make me feel needed even when I'm fully absorbed in my work, be it his bouncing rubber ball dropped at my feet or his long impatient sigh alerting me that our walk for the day is long overdue; Buddy has won over my heart.

Affection is defined as "a fond attachment, devotion, or love." (Webster's)

When Buddy underwent surgery two days ago, a pool of affection formed deep in my heart.

Now back home, Bud's recovering well, and sad but true, Steve and I were told that if the tumors on his body are indeed malignant, even chemotherapy won't help.

Looking into his groggy eyes that day, I cupped Buddy's furry face in my hands and gently kissed the tip of his nose.

"I love you, Bud," I whispered, "and if you are sick in some way, I don't want to know."

Buddy affectionately wagged his tail. We were fully in agreement.

Things We Can Learn From A Dog

1. Never pass up the opportunity to go for a joy ride.

2. Allow the experience of fresh air & the wind in your face to be pure ecstasy.

3. When loved ones come home, always run to greet them.

4. When it's in your best interest, practice obedience.

5. Let others know when they've invaded your territory.

6. Take naps & stretch before rising.

7. Run, romp & play daily.

8. Eat with gusto & enthusiasm.

9. Be Loyal.

10. Never pretend to be something you're not.

11. If what you want lies buried, dig until you find it.

12. When someone is having a bad day, be silent, sit close by & nuzzle them gently.

13. Thrive on attention & let people touch you.

14. Avoid biting when a simple growl will do.

15. On hot days, drink lots of water & lay under a shady tree.

16. When you're happy, dance around & wag your entire body.

17. No matter how often you're scolded, don't buy into the guilt thing & pout. — Run right back and make friends.

18. Bond with your pack.

19. Delight in the simple joy of a long walk.

~Author Unknown

ETE = Enjoy the Experience™
Lesson learned June 21, (year 2)

LEARNING THE ROPES

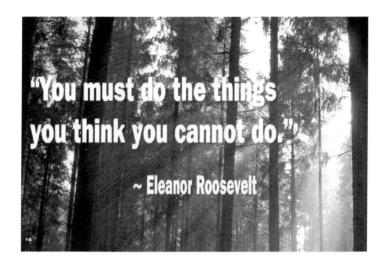

"You must do the things you think you cannot do."

~ Eleanor Roosevelt

I've been much more joyfully curious and appreciatively accepting this week.

Steve and I awoke on Sunday and agreed to head up to the beautiful Kootenai National Forest.

After sharing a plateful of scrambled eggs and a piece of buttered toast, we jumped on the Gold Wing and braved the cool morning weather.

Brisk winds pushed us toward the Cabinet Mountain range as our chilly bodies slowly warmed with the sun.

It was one breathtaking snapshot after another: a spectacular ride across the 2400+ ft. Lake Koocanusa bridge; a mountainous panoramic view of the Idaho, Montana & Canadian borders; and a colorful rainbow trellis peaking through the crystal waters of the Yaak River Falls.

It was beauty at its best and a great warm up trip for our upcoming fundraising Ride for Hope next month.

Just a few days later, I joined a group of 11 from the resort for a fun two and a half hour trek in the trees. I had no idea what to expect. I only was told to dress in comfortable hiking gear.

Imagine my surprise when three outdoor guides brought us to a training camp, partnered us up, fitted us with climbing gear and told us to practice belaying from one "pretend" tree to another.

As I tightened the safety harness around my waist and thighs, nervous energy began to build amongst the group.

?

- What was I getting myself into now?
- Would I be strong or give my fear away?
- Could I really face my fear of heights?

"Just be sure you work together as a team," a guide advised.

I made sure to make a mental note of it as we hiked up a ½ mile trail and stopped at a man-made ladder in the middle of the woods.

I cautiously looked up to see several 2-by-4's suspended side-by-side in the walk through the treetops which consisted of a 700 foot boardwalk connected by several cables that hung from tree-to-tree

"Our job is to safely get across," a second guide said.

"When you step down it's going to feel like you're walking on a boat floating in water," a third one added

The resort's Sales Manager nervously took her first step onto the swaying bridge and "clipped in," as they say.

"Ahhh," she shrieked as her knees began to buckle. "This is bloody ridiculous."

My partner, Terry, began to tremble.

"I'm scared," she said, turning her face back to me and the two guys at the rear.

Photo courtesy of Ron Mallery

I carefully leaned over and cupped her face in my hands.

"Terry," I assured her. "You're just excited. You're not scared."

"You're just excited," I repeated. "Now keep telling yourself that, because we need to get across."

Terry gulped then courageously nodded.

She lifted herself onto the platform and extended her first crab claw out toward the cable.

"Yellow on belay," she quavered.

"Belay on," I confirmed. "You're doing great."

How was it I was being so calm?

Once Terry's ropes were securely fastened, I hoisted myself up and took my first step onto one of the oscillating boards.

Just as the guide had instructed, it began to swing under foot.

AHHH! Inexperienced climbers are called "gumby's," but I felt more like a bird that had just overindulged in the fermented berries of the mountain ash trees . . . Talk about a drunk, distorted feeling!

Terry grimaced from up ahead. I looked up just on time to see a dangling steel cable snag her perched sunglasses right off her head.

They plummeted then crashed more than 50 feet below.

"Breathe in the nose and breathe out the mouth," I said to Terry. Was I really convincing her or me?

Belay on. Belay off.

Higher and higher we went until we were suspended to the full 70 feet in the air.

I breathed a big sigh of relief! I did it. I really did it!!

As I pulled myself up the last ascending ramp, a guy behind me thought it would be funny to start jumping up and down to celebrate.

The boards became so unbalanced I had to do everything I could to keep a steady grip. Mind you, we are all connected, and by this time Terry was wobbling to and fro and somehow managed to traverse to the highest platform where she then got brave and started jumping back.

I was monkey in the middle of a flimsy floored teeter totter, and let me tell you the inclining wobble was so steep that I was at the end of my rope (literally!)

The jolt of each jump pulled my safety harness tighter and tighter until I was nearly lifted off my feet by my crotch.

"That's enough please," I pleaded as I yanked at the riding rope. "I feel like I'm being split in half."

The two kept laughing and jumping, when suddenly a plank beneath our feet abruptly busted off the nearest tree.

Crrrack!!

Terry began to scream.

A guide in front of us started shouting, as the "jokester" behind me stopped frozen in his tracks. We now were all balancing on just a couple of boards.

Surprisingly, I was still remaining calm.

Perhaps I was just in shock?

By the time we were safely on the ground, Terry addressed me to the group, "I watched you when that board broke, Michelle, and you didn't even yell. You just stood there like everything was fine."

I couldn't help but smile.

Had this happened even three years ago, I would have seriously screamed my head off and then started madly crying and going into a panic attack.

And then when the board broke, I would have fallen to my knees and crazily envisioned my body crashing beneath the trees and the only way to get me down would have been to pry me off the remaining boards.

My, how far I've come!

It's difficult to even put this into words.

Though the word fearless seemed a bit fitting for this experience, God tells me I was "an intrepid spirit" that day.

Intrepid means "resolutely fearless"

**Resolutely means "set in purpose;
characterized by firmness and determination,
as the spirit, temper, actions, etc." (Webster's)**

I'm very much enjoying this new me!

ETE = Enjoy the Experience™
Lesson learned June 21, (year 2)

GIVE YOUR SELF A FRESH START

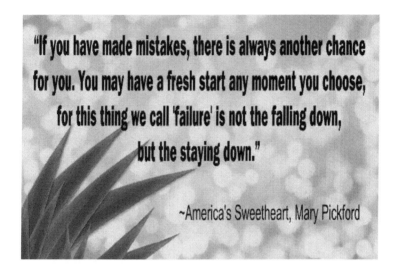

"If you have made mistakes, there is always another chance for you. You may have a fresh start any moment you choose, for this thing we call 'failure' is not the falling down, but the staying down."

~America's Sweetheart, Mary Pickford

This week winter has spring spinning with confusion as snow and hail greet the ground.

It's been pretty fascinating watching fresh blankets of powder cover the lawn again and again and again, each time followed by sunshine that melts it all away.

These recent weather patterns remind me a lot of the stress cycle that constantly replays in our life until something else occurs that can bring the situation back to light.

A few days ago I spoke to a group of business professionals about this quite a bit.

"Just how does one remain calm during stressful situations?" I asked the participants.

The group began to discuss the many events that will often trigger a negative response.

"Take the weather for example," I said.

"Let's say the sun hasn't shined in awhile.

How does this event make you feel?

Or, shall I say. How do you make your Self feel?

Though you may not like to hear it, you are in control of how you feel with every occurrence in your life, and though you can allow it to negatively affect your entire day, is that really the outcome that you desire?"

Most everyone in the group shook their head 'no'.

"Regardless of the situation," I continued, "always ask your Self, 'How does this thought make me feel?'

"See your response as an opportunity to take a look at your life from a glowing new perspective.

In other words, give your Self a FRESH START!"

Fresh means "newly made." Start means a "beginning." (Webster's).

Newly made beginnings are part of your gifts of choice.

Every day you get to choose how to respond.

So, what's your view of the world?

Are we in a falling recession, or is this finally our chance to get some really good deals?

Is the rising cost of fuel pure tragedy, or rather a wonderful opportunity to "Go Green?"

Do you fear falling sick with a disease or the flu, or instead welcome wellness with healing thoughts and positive energy?

Are you eating each bite feeling guilty of your weight, or are you fully aware and appreciative of your food?

Do you fill your brain with confusing controversy (like all the drama on TV?), or do you remember that your subconscious doesn't know the difference between fantasy and reality and so you carefully choose what you watch, how you feel, and what you do?

Whether it's a dark blanket of clouds covering up the sun, another spring snowfall, or an opportunity to react to that which life presents, Fresh Starts are always good!

Choose to be fully aware and awake by consciously moving your Self out of the conditioned negative thought patterns and toward a newly made beginning of light.

Simple Steps:
Start by becoming aware of your perspective.

- Turn your Self-talk into words that will nurture rather than words that will hurt.
- Begin to look at the world with a fresh pair of eyes, and ask your Self "What can I do to fully control the situation?"
- Trust your intuition then give it a whirl.
- If it feels right, then it is.
- And, remember, Enjoy the Experience™ come what may!

ETE = Enjoy the Experience™
Lesson learned March 29, (year 2)

HOW LOW CAN YOU GO?

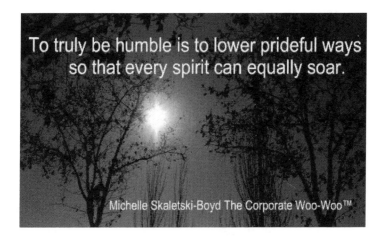

To truly be humble is to lower prideful ways
so that every spirit can equally soar.

Michelle Skaletski-Boyd The Corporate Woo-Woo™

I've been thinking a lot about humble lately and wondering what it means.

To be humble means to be "modest and not arrogant"

My ego likes the sound of that, but, hold the boastful boat!

To be humble also means to be "lowly" and "to have a feeling of insignificance and inferiority." (Webster's)

I don't know about your ego, but my ego is putting up a lot of resistance right now.

Does this mean being humble really means we're expected to lower ourselves to the point of losing Self-dignity and societal respect and position?

Just the mere thought of this is causing me to want to put up a fight.

But, hold on a second. There may be another way . . .

What happens if I set my pride aside and become fully aware of my essential Self?

Ahhh. Now I get it.

Status is nothing more than an illusion. We can't take it with us when we die, so spiritually speaking we all stand on equal ground.

On the other hand though, isn't it true that some people live with false pretenses and do whatever it takes to appear powerful, while others believe that the nail that sticks up is only asking to be hammered down, and so they make excuses for their God-given talents so as not to be perceived as prevailing?

This is soooo confusing!

Deception and apologizing are more make-believe than modesty, are they not?

And, what about those who choose to term success as the Tall Poppy Syndrome saying overachievement deserves public dishonor and degradation?

Do individuals who stand out from the crowd really deserve to be "cut down to size" just like the tallest poppy in the garden?

Isn't reducing someone with insult and injury just as bad as conceited bragging and boasting?

Am I the only one who stays up and thinks about these things?

Seriously, when it comes to being humble, just where do we draw the line?

I know back in my 20's, when I was out of work, I needed to take a job as an asphalt sealer just to pay the bills. The work was demeaning, (my nickname was 'tar monkey") not to mention extremely difficult. And though my ego felt really degraded at the time, looking back I can honestly say my spirit knew otherwise.

It was one of the most humbling things I ever did to survive.

Humble and humiliate are both derived from the Latin word humus which means 'ground'.

Therefore, it's in my "humble" opinion that being humble has nothing to do with physical form such as whether you're a 'tall poppy' or not. It simply means lowering your spirit so it moves to a place of deeper ground.

Because when you get too hung up in caring about how you look to the world, you resist your true place and experience painful humiliation because you illusively go off and 'lose' your pride.

No one is truly humble when their egos are boasting about wealth and fame, pretending to be someone they're not, cutting others down in hopes of feeling better, or pretending to be less than they are.

To truly be humble is to lower prideful ways so that every spirit can equally soar.

ETE = Enjoy the Experience™
Lesson learned April 12 (year 2)

WHEN CHOICE IS UNCLEAR

"We have to believe in freewill. We've got no choice." ~Isaac Bashevis Singer, Nobel prize winner

I like this funny quote in the image above. It's my freewill to choose it, and I'm sticking to it!

Freewill means "based on our own accord," and accord means "to be in harmony; agreement." (Webster's)

Thus, having freewill is having harmony with your Self and feeling good about your decisions. And though you don't always get what you want, you do always get a choice in your reaction.

In other words, even when there are obstacles, you're able to decide mentally, physically, spiritually &/or intellectually how you'll choose to react and what will be your next move.

My friend, Joanne, and I had a conversation that was centered around freewill just the other day. We had agreed to meet in downtown Spokane, Washington. I had been there for a keynote speech that I had delivered at the historical and beautiful Davenport Hotel.

And since we were both getting off work around the same time, we agreed to meet for happy hour at the downtown mall.

The last time we spoke, Joanne's inner-voice had been persistently reminding her that she needed to quit her job and spend more time as a photographer, so I was anxious to catch up with her.

"Well?" I prompted, "What's going on with your job situation?"

"I told my employer they may want to start looking for my replacement," Joanne beamed.

"Congratulations!" I cheered.

Joanne began to smile and then impatiently sighed, "Thanks. I'm happy with my choice, but ever since I've given notice, obstacle after obstacle has begun to appear."

I lovingly grinned, as I fully related.

"My brother," she explained, "who is also my roommate, just had emergency surgery and now needs homecare assistance, so I'm now a nurse by day and a nurse by night. So, other than ordering new camera equipment last week, there's been no more room for photography in my life."

"Isn't it something how we're tested by the Universe to see if we're going to lose our focus?" I empathized.

"Yes," Joanne said, "and I know I'm going to get where I want to be, but it's taking longer than I thought."

We chatted about this for awhile.

Joanne knows that true commitment means never looking back. Whenever your mind gets set on a new direction, your freewill changes, so it's extremely likely that obstacles will be involved.

It's much like pulling up an anchor and then discovering you can't take off until you first deal with all of the remnants attached.

There will be muck and seaweed and many other crazy entanglements way before you can ever set sail.

And all this work is why so many people throw the anchor back in and stay right where they are, because they'd rather feel helpless than deal with all the crud.

I reminded Joanne of this when it was time to part ways. "Just keep trusting your goal no matter how turned around you might get."

"Will do," she said with conviction.

Two days later, I found myself questioning the reason why remnants remain.

God answered by pointing my eyes to a pile of dried up pine needles that had fallen beneath the trees.

Should the trees focus on their shedding or on their growth?

"On their growth," I mentally replied.

Is shedding part of growth?

"Yes."

This is your answer.

Another lesson learned!

Just as trees cast off their needles in order to grow, change for the better requires persistence and patience during times of separation.

You can either put all of your attention on the loss or keep some of your focus for the gain.

Freewill is harmony, so do what you please.

ETE = Enjoy the Experience™
Lesson learned April 26, (year 2)

SHAPESHIFTING

"You already possess everything necessary to become great."

~ Crow

Steve and I are riding out for our motorcycle fundraiser today. The weather is said to reach over 90 degrees.

I'm looking forward to clearing my head.

I've hit some murky waters this past week. A surge of busyness has caused me to slack on working on an important project, so I've been playing the "skip one week and then frantically catch up" game.

I'm looking forward to things starting to settle soon.

Being up at the land last weekend was a very wild experience!

I had just built a little campfire and was sitting at the picnic table preparing for a speech when a "Bambi"

deer flew by through the forest, as if it were running for its life.

My immediate instinct was to think something was hot on its trail.

I slowly turned my head, and, there, not even 20 yards away stood a timber wolf.

Its grey, white and black fur-covered body stopped suddenly in its tracks.

"It's a wolf," I quietly gasped to Steve. Then, just as quickly as I could, I bolted toward the truck.

Steve instructed Buddy to lie down and to stay. The last thing we needed was for those two dogs to tangle.

The beautiful wolf perked its ears back and cautiously maneuvered its way around the woodpile to see if there was another way through.

No such luck.

Looking despaired, it slowly circled out the same way it came in.

My heart was racing like mad.

This was a mind bending experience!

My rushing adrenaline allowed me to think about nothing else the remainder of the evening.

Wolves symbolize intuition, knowledge and instinct, as well as death, destruction and deceit.

It seems like a complete contradiction.

I began to wonder why.

A few days later, I took Buddy for a walk and fell into deep meditation.

Several magpies flew overhead, reminding me of the constant shift between darkness and light.

A moment later, a flock of crows began to loudly cackle then flew upward toward the trees.

Just like the wolf, crows can be conniving in nature with an uncanny ability to teach us life lessons, even through trickery.

Wolves and crows have both virtues and vices, and both represent transformation.

Just like the wolf and the crow, I've been feeling myself moving through negative and positive energy as my spirit continues to shapeshift.

Shape is "an assumed appearance."
Shift means "to put aside and replace it by
another." (Webster's)

Spiritual shapeshifting is the ability to positively transform consciousness. Most importantly, it means never allowing your true Self to become stagnant.

You might say, it's purification at its best.

As one becomes more and more spiritually awakened, it's like adding water to a never-ending fish tank.

As the level of our consciousness peacefully rises, the depth of our being expands.

It's a refreshing and renewing experience!

The more we awaken, the more we rise to the top and become closer to the light.

So, why is it that things can sometimes look so dim?

Because trickery comes into play. Every time a conscious shift occurs, the bottom of our "tank" gets disturbed.

Negative energies and fearful "crud" float to the surface of our mind, creating cloudy and murky waters for a while.

Thankfully the wolf and the crows were keen enough to shift in to remind me of this.

ETE = Enjoy the Experience™
Lesson learned July 26, (year 2)

CADENCES OF LIFE

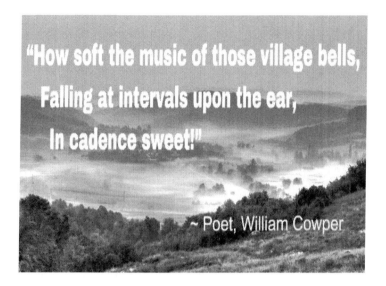

"How soft the music of those village bells,
Falling at intervals upon the ear,
In cadence sweet!"

~ Poet, William Cowper

While attending a symphony event with Steve last weekend I gave some thought about the cadences of life.

Cadence is defined as "the flow or rhythm of events, especially the pattern in which something is experienced." (Webster's)

As we took our seats up in the balcony, I glanced at the Arabian Nights' program guide just as the lights went dim.

The theme of the concert focused on a Persian Queen named Scheherazade whose life was spared because of her gifted ability to story tell.

As the conductor took his place on stage, Scheherazade's fascinating stories came to life.

A stern brass section represented the sultan King who would come to decide if Scheherazade's life would come to conclusion or be spared.

Also in cadence, was Scheherazade's sweet voice floating freely through the weaving tales of the woodwinds, telling sinuous stories about Sinbad and the sea.

Each ebb and flow of the story rocked the audience in a cradle of ocean waves, keeping the fictional sultan and his followers at the very edges of their seats.

And so the story goes, Scheherazade was saved from execution because of her clever ability to create a suspending segue to each and every 1,001 Arabian stories and tales.

This helped me discover cadence has many chords.

Just like the song of life, your melodic experiences can be very strong or very weak.

A weak cadence has no root in its position.

This happens when you whimsically float through life without any rhyme or reason. It's when you get so busy with daily routine you hypnotically move through the world unaware and unawake.

An authentic cadence is one in which to master. It means taking the time to be fully aware of your goals by recognizing where you are now in the moment and where you are desiring to be.

Life is an ever changing sheet of music — some notes are eruptive — some tranquil and sweet.

?

- Do you hold each moment in such fascination and anticipation that every turn of life becomes appreciatively tuneful?
- Is your personal cadence magically authentic or imperfectly weak?
- Are you fully aware of your sequential sound?

Spend time daily becoming mindful of your unique melodious sounds.

Ask your Self: Where am I going? Where have I been?

Life is a musical masterpiece.

How does your cadence sound?

ETE = Enjoy the Experience™
Lesson learned March 1, (year 2)

REFLECTING BACK AT ME

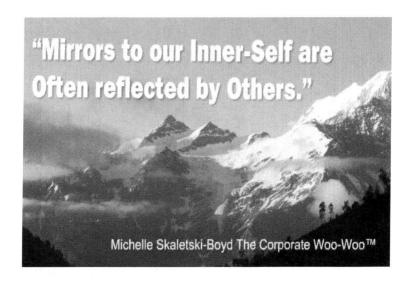

"Mirrors to our Inner-Self are Often reflected by Others."

Michelle Skaletski-Boyd The Corporate Woo-Woo™

Being tucked in the snow-capped mountains is like living inside of a postcard.

It's a dream come true!

What a wonderful December this has been. Calling home and hearing the voices of family and friends brought us all together again.

And, the greatest thing of all is that it's been exactly one year since Steve and I first stepped foot into our new home. I remember how nervous I was moving into a house I had never even seen.

Now we're here acclimating to the new weather conditions, making new friends and starting new traditions. We've been so very blessed.

Speaking of joyous blessings, Steve and I volunteered our time at a soup kitchen not too far from home.

It was the start of our holiday and also the beginning of our learning the intricate art of giving and receiving.

Though we went to the kitchen believing others were the ones in need, Steve and I left filled with memories of happy smiles and gratitude. The simple gift of offering a cup of coffee to a cold weary soul filled our hearts with love, and by the next morning, my husband was as giddy as a little boy.

"It's Christmas" he squealed, "Come on. Let's get up. Let's go open our presents. Come on!"

He tossed back the covers and flew out of bed.

I couldn't believe how excited he was. I hadn't seen anything like it since I was a little kid. My little sister and brother used to do the very same thing.

"Merry Christmas," I softly whispered then pulled the covers over my head. "I need to sleep in a little longer please."

"No, No, No," Steve moaned, "It's time to get up. Really. Come on! Come on!"

He jiggled the bed. "It's time to open preeeeeesents!!"

I squinted at the clock. Red blurry numbers glared back at me. (Ugh. I have never been a morning person.)

"Are you serious?" I groaned.

Yes. Get up. I'll start breakfast."

The very idea of food caused me to perk right up.

"Okay," I smiled.

Steve knows a home cooked morning meal gets me every time!

I sat up slowly and stretched toward my toes.

It's really Christmas. It's really here!

A year ago we were waking up on the floor of our old farmhouse. All of our furniture was packed in a moving trailer — even our bed.

Now the smell of bacon wafted through the house.

A fresh blanket of snow covered the ground and magnificent magic filled the air.

What a wonderful year this has been!

Consider taking a moment to reflect on how things are going in your world.

Reflection is defined as "careful consideration" and "fixing your thoughts on something." (Webster's)

Reflection is a powerful creation.

When you look in the mirror, what do you see?

A true reflection reveals One Being in Perfect Light.

This is a law of the universe called The Law of Reflection.

It's a radiant ray of incoming light and a radiant outgoing beam. Both meet simultaneously at exactly the same place, the same time and the same angle.

They are mirror images of one another acting as perfect reflections of light.

You're a beautiful creation indeed!

ETE = Enjoy the Experience™
Lesson learned on Dec 29, (year 1)

SPIRITUAL TRANSFORMATION AND ADAPTATION

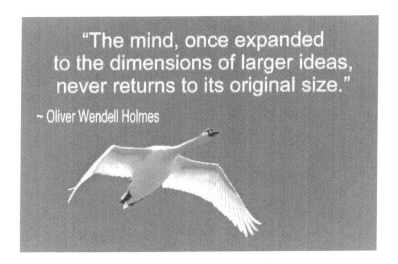

"The mind, once expanded
to the dimensions of larger ideas,
never returns to its original size."

~ Oliver Wendell Holmes

I spent the first full day of spring inside the Glacier National Park where I spotted a graceful and elegant swan.

It is said that the swan is a symbol of transformation and for surrendering to the power of the Great Spirit. When spotted, it is said to assist with accepting one's ability to know what lies ahead and to keep paying attention to one's internal intuition.

How absolutely fitting given I met with my fertility specialist this week.

Even though I couldn't help but place a little hope on the remaining 1% chance of finally getting pregnant, my quiet meditation last week led me to believe that I was reaching for something that just wasn't meant to be.

Since then I've undergone some major shifts in my being.

A couple of years ago, when Steve and I received a message that adoption was an option, deep down we still believed we'd be able to conceive a baby with no problems on our own.

These past few days, however, I've come to feel differently now.

At this point in life, Steve and I are clearly being presented the chance to experience something not many individuals ever get to face.

How many people are put in a position where they must seriously consider adopting or fostering in order to have a child in their life? And how many have to face the fact that they may be without children for the duration of their life?

Even in the board game called LIFE your chances of landing on a "baby boy" space or "baby girl" space are really pretty good.

People just go on their merry little way in their little plastic cars while adding their blue pegged boys and pink pegged girls, not really giving much thought as to why they landed on the spaces that they did.

But for some reason after Steve and I chose the "Get Married" path, the spinner skipped us on the baby part.

Perhaps that's because every time we landed on an "Adoption" space, we put the pedal to the metal and gave the wheel another go???

Mind you, we have nothing against fostering or adoption. In fact, for the longest time, we thought of them as two wonderful alternatives. We even put our names on a waiting list back in the Midwest for a child classified by the system as "special needs."

Contrary to what most people think, a special needs child doesn't necessarily mean one with physical disabilities. Though this can be one factor of several considerations, most special needs children are older and beyond the toddler stage.

Perhaps they have brothers and sisters. Perhaps they've experienced trauma in some dramatic way and now need more love to help heal the pain.

Regardless of their situation, there are many special needs children in this world just hoping and praying for a family who will offer them love and consistency, yet sadly they're bypassed and often overlooked.

Even after moving to the mountains, Steve and I explored the special needs fostering and adopting path, yet we continued to remain hopeful that we'd get pregnant on our own.

But, God works in mysterious ways.

Over the course of the past seven years our spirits just kept-on-a shifting.

Despite these strong spiritual pulls, our stubborn pride kept getting in the way, preventing us from fully following its light. You might even say we've been sitting in the dark with just a little flashlight unable to admit until now that the "get pregnant' batteries have been drained.

Since seeing the fertility specialist, I've become awakened to the truth of something Steve taught me long ago. - It's time to 'Improvise, Adapt, and Overcome', because we have no other choice at this point.

We'll improvise by giving up on the idea of conception. In order to do this, we must adapt.

Adapt means "to adjust or modify fittingly; to make suitable to conditions." (Webster's)

Now that I've learned my physical body is simply not wired to have a child, it will be important to adapt emotionally, intellectually and spiritually so that all pieces of my Self become fully aligned and complete.

Like all stages of personal adaptation, this will involve shifting my thoughts, my perceptions and my personal beliefs about the world of adoption and about me.

Adaptation number one is realizing that not being able to conceive a child doesn't mean I'm less of a woman or undeserving in any way. It simply means I'm being called to fulfill a duty that not many women are ever asked to fulfill.

(Yes, I'm talking to myself right now or shall I say my Self is talking to me.)

Adaptation number two is being stronger than ever and having the courage to face whatever comes my way.

Adaptation number three is learning to trust God's plan completely while setting aside any fears so that nature's calling can be answered.

Thanks to the swan, I now understand it is time to follow the Divine so completely that I begin to adapt and surrender to anything I'm asked to overcome!

ETE = Enjoy the Experience™
Lesson learned March 22, (year 2)

CONFIDENCE REMAINS

"If I have lost confidence in myself
I have the universe against me."

~ Ralph Waldo Emerson

This quotation definitely explains some things.

Personally, when I lose my confidence I feel completely off-center.

I get stuck in a pity-pot feeling sorry for myself, yet I often don't recognize it.

I was in that pitiful pot this week.

I began to think about how it's nearing autumn and how I still haven't grown my business to the size I want it to be.

I began to fear I've been my wasting time living out a dream that may turn out to be a dead-end.

My ego was at the wheel again which some say means E.dging G.od O.ut yet I'd prefer to think of it more as 'Everyone's Got One'

And though the Divine is always omnipresent, when it's just you and God and no one else you can sometimes feel like you're all alone.

Unbeknownst to me, as I walked Buddy through the park the other day, I was about to be taught a very valuable lesson.

There we were playing fetch when my Golden Retriever began sniffing around as if to relieve him self (and I'm not talking the liquid contents kind).

Just as he began to squat, a neighbor appeared just a couple of yards away.

Embarrassment spread across my face as I wondered how I'd be judged.

I evaluated quickly.

Hurry it up Dog, I thought

Thank goodness the trees were still blocking the neighbor's view.

- What happens if he sees?
- What would he think of me?
- Would I be expected to scoop up my dog's poo right then and there?

How humiliating that would be.

Seconds felt like minutes, and after what felt like forever Buddy finished his doggy duty (pun intended) just as the neighbor man appeared.

Wanting to block all evidence, I took a step back.

"It looks like it might rain," the neighbor man called out.

"We sure need it," I said forcing a smile and stepping back again.

The neighbor waved to me and then power-walked past me saying, "Have a great day!"

Oh my goodness.

Talk about a close call!

Now it was time to clean up the mess.

I took a step toward the park's "clean up after your pets" pedestal to retrieve a doggy doo bag when I noticed my right shoe felt like it was stuck in a clump of mud.

I balanced myself on my left leg and flipped my right shoe over to have myself a look, and would you believe my shoe was caked with Buddy's poo?!!

Can you believe I had stepped in my own dog's doo?!! (Just goes to show how I still care too much about what other's think.)

Worse yet, after dragging my heel across the lawn like a freak, I begrudgingly discovered all the doggy doo bags were gone.

What a day I was having!

Buddy began to wag his tail.

I found nothing funny about it.

I pulled some tissues from my pocket and used them to pick up the left-overs from the lawn.

How totally disgusting this was!

Then I scraped my shoe on every stick and every rock I could find.

It was way more gross than I can describe.

When I got home I kicked off my shoes in the garage and padded my stocking feet up the stairs.

I told Steve what happened, and he began to laugh hysterically.

"The funniest thing is you were trying to avoid the very thing you attracted," he said.

I was still not smiling.

As I wallowed my way into my office, God gently chuckled and said.

Find your confidence again and you'll be okay.

At this point I was up for anything, so I pulled out my dictionary.

Confidence.

Confidence is defined as "full trust; belief in the powers." (Webster's)

It was then I realized that my second guessing everything, such as caring so much about what the neighbor might think, was causing me to separate my Self from the Universe. And, I didn't like its remains.

— Another lesson learned.

ETE = Enjoy the Experience™
Lesson learned on Sept 01, (year 1)

LOVE BIRDS

"Throw your dreams into space like a kite,
And you do not know what it will bring back,
A new life, a new friend, a new love,
A new country."

~ Anais Nin

Being in the mountains now is like living the best of both worlds.

There's been fluffy snow in the morning and 40 degree sunshine by mid-afternoon.

It was Valentine's Day on Thursday, and though not everyone celebrates this day, I personally spent quite a bit of time anticipating this big LOVE day.

Perhaps it's because Steve and I haven't had a vacation in nearly two years, or because we both jumped into a new state and new jobs so fast that our relationship has been filled with strain.

Whatever the reason, I truly began to believe that Steve would surprise me with something very romantic on Valentine's Day. I even hinted quite a bit, letting him know I needed him to woo me more, though I realize now that hinting doesn't count.

As many females do, I had envisioned my honey waking me up and offering me a loving foot massage while feeding me chocolate covered strawberries and white sparkling champagne.

I know. I know. It's a little silly really, but a girl can dream, can't she?

In reality, Steve slept in longer than usual then rushed off to work.

I was rather disappointed given I was all set to receive, yet deep down I knew I was being selfish given he had to work, and I could sleep in.

My ego, however, honestly believed Steve was still going to surprise me in some way, and so I spent the day cleaning, cooking, baking, shoveling and "setting the stage" for the big romantic night so as not to be outdone.

(Notice the crumbling "intention" of the foundation that was obviously doomed from the start.)

By mid-afternoon, the smell of homemade spaghetti was permeating the room. Fresh oatmeal raisin cookies were packaged up in a bright shiny heart-covered bag, and next to it was a mushy mylar balloon held in place by an "I Love You" string attached to a sentimental greeting card.

Still no call from Steve.

I began to wonder if he had forgotten me, so I picked up the phone to let him know dinner was ready and to also confirm our plans for the night.

I could tell by all the background noise that he was busy.

"Happy Valentine's Day, by the way, " he said, just before we both hung up. "Your card is in my nightstand in the bedroom."

I began to sigh as I hung up the phone.

Is this really what marriage is like after 10 years? I have to go dig out my own card?

Though a part of me wanted to cry, I had just applied my makeup. (seriously.)

I inhaled deeply, knowing I had a choice . . .

I could either pop the balloon, tear up the card, and eat all the cookies, or I could try the neutral approach and see how it went as hard as it may be.

By the time Steve arrived home, I had eaten 3 cookies (really), and my mind was a mess. Part of me was upset, yet another part remained hopeful that something good would come out of this night.

"You seem upset," Steve observed as he came up the stairs and pecked me on the lips.

"No, I'm just running behind," I said, forcing a smile.

"No worries," Steve encouraged. "Is there anything I can do?"

"No thanks," I replied. "I just don't want to be late."

I shut off the stove, presuming the spaghetti noodles were cooked, but when I put them in the strainer, they were still a little hard.

"Ahhhh," I cried. "This is not turning out as I had hoped."

Thinking quickly, Steve grabbed a plastic container, flipped the noodles into it, and then put a lid on it so they could steam.

"I tell you what," Steve suggested, "How about we eat after we get home?"

I glanced at the clock.

"Okay," I said, "but I know this event is not something you really want to do, so promise me you won't be cranky because you haven't eaten yet and please don't complain, okay?"

"Promise," Steve assured.

Though I was honestly a bit hesitant and uncertain about how Steve would react to the night I had planned, I was very much looking forward to getting out.

Steve drove us to a neighboring town then held my hand as we walked into the building. (brownie points!!)

The meeting room was packed. There must have been more than 60 people there.

The speaker began with a Native American sage smudging ceremony that was said to dispel the room of any evil energies. I inhaled deeply and watched as Steve carefully took the handmade bowl in his left hand and cupped the herb-scented air with his right. He then waved the thick smoke of the sage over his entire body and handed the bowl to me.

I was quite impressed, as I had forgotten he had performed this ritual many times when he worked as a security guard for a Native American tribe back in Wisconsin.

I followed my husband's lead, asking God to please clear away any negative energy that might yet be lingering between us.

A few minutes later the lead facilitator struck a beautiful singing bowl with his leather wrapped mallet. It was one of the most beautiful sounds I have ever heard.

Its harmonic overtones filled the room.

We were all told we were to connect to our sacred selves and then ask for a vision from above.

The facilitator began playing a hypnotic CD that was said to assist in relaxation.

"Please close your eyes," he proclaimed, "and allow your mind to go where it will."

I inhaled deeply and began to meditate.

Are you there, God?

I'm always with you, Michelle.

Please show me a sign so I know Steve and I are going to be okay.

Within seconds a beautiful bird appeared. It was the most fantastic creature I have ever seen.

The entire body was filled with every color of the rainbow, and though it seems impossible, it appeared to be smiling at me.

Then, a majestic waterfall came to mind. It was as if I was standing under it and embraced in the arms of Steve. We were joyous and happy and in love.

Moments later the facilitator called us back to our present surroundings, and I couldn't help but wonder what my vision could possibly mean.

On our car ride back home, I turned to my hubby and asked, "Did you get any type of vision?"

"I saw a lot of purple," he said, "but I don't meditate as much as you, so everything looked like a blob."

I began to laugh.

"I saw the most beautiful colored bird," I said. "I don't even know how to describe it other than to say it was fascinating to me. Then, I saw us holding each other under a waterfall. It was so purifying and so serene."

"That sounds nice," Steve smiled.

Since then, a couple of days have passed, and I have asked God for some further assistance in interpreting what it all means.

He guided me to use the internet.

Though I knew Native American tradition teaches that visions are to be interpreted by the receiver, what I had not yet known was that the color purple is said to represent very spiritual thoughts.

I also learned that my "rainbow bird" is a native of Australia called a rainbow lorikeet and can live to be 20 years, and, get this . . . this precious colorful bird chooses a mate for life!

Awww!

So, even though I never did get a foot rub or those decadent strawberries and champagne, I did get this even greater gift — absolute certainty that a spiritual ascension with my husband is exactly where I belong!

Ascend means "to move, climb, or go upward; to go toward the source or beginning." (Webster's)

ETE = Enjoy the Experience™
Lesson learned February 16, (year 2)

About The Author

The Corporate Woo-Woo™
Michelle Skaletski-Boyd

At a very young age, I began communicating with a Higher Power, who referred to Himself as 'God.' I was soon introduced to my guardian angels and other heavenly guides.

Still too young to understand intuition, I shared my experiences with a religious relative who warned me not to listen. I then grew fearful and conflicted, secretly wondering if the "voices in my head" were more dissociative than divine.

Growing up in a family of 5, I was raised strict Roman Catholic, so being true to my Self didn't always come naturally. Had it not been for my maternal grandmother who followed the customs and traditions of Cherokee ways I may not have gained the skill sets or the courage to be sharing my soul gifts today.

I know first hand what it's like to live in a world where everything feels off, to spin in hopelessness, and to stay stuck in upset and grief. For many years I learned to silence my sounds of intuition, becoming so disconnected from my Higher Self that my insides turned angry and depressed. After graduating cum laude from a private college, I gained a lot of experience in the Corporate world, even teaching part-time at the college level, all the while secretly fearing what would happen if I put my Self out there. Would others think I was crazy or nuts or weird? That's why today I make fun of these feelings by titling myself the Corporate Woo-Woo™

So, if you're ready to become more Self empowered, are willing to do your own inner-work to strengthen your intuition, and are ready to connect more fully to your Higher Self, then I just may be the intuitive guide for you.

Namaste,
Michelle

More Books By The Corporate Woo-Woo™: Best-Seller, **Words for the Soul: Heaven-Sent Life Lessons & Conversations with God, Volume 2**

Questions For The Author?
Email: **tech@soul-felt.com**

Want to lift your spirits and challenge your thinking? Sign up for a free gift at **http://www.soul-felt.com/**

Interested in Scheduling Private Soul Sessions?
Email **tech@soul-felt.com**

One More Thing . . .

If you believe this book contains some powerful messages, I would appreciate it if you would take a moment to share it with your friends. I personally know spiritual short stories can make a huge difference in someone's life, so I would be most grateful if you also posted a positive review on Amazon.

A soul-felt thank you!
Enjoy the Experience™

Made in the USA
San Bernardino, CA
09 February 2016